JUST JU-JITSU

JUST
JU-JITSU

Ken Cole

The Crowood Press

First published in 2006 by
The Crowood Press Ltd
Ramsbury, Marlborough
Wiltshire SN8 2HR

www.crowood.com

British Library Cataloguing-in-Publication Data
A catalogue record for this book is available from the British Library.

ISBN   1 86126 849 1
EAN   978 1 86126 849 5

Acknowledgements
Many thanks to my wife San, my photographer and proofreader, and my
willing helpers/victims in said photographs: Lee, Chris, Paul, Mike and
Richard.
    Thanks to *Sensei* Eric Marshall and his knuckle-walkers: Paul D.,
Gary M., Dougie, Stan, Garry H., Ronnie, Martin B., Stewart H., Paul
B., Geoff C. and others with whom I spent many an interesting training
session.
    Thanks to *Sensei* Arthur Bradley for his support whilst I have been
down in the Midlands.
    Finally a special thanks to the *Ren Shin Kan Aikido* Club for the loan
of their excellent *dojo* as a setting for the photographs.

Photography by Sandra Cole.
Kanji calligraphy by the author.

Disclaimer
Please note that the author and the publisher of this book are not
responsible in any manner whatsoever for any damage or injury of any
kind that might result from practising and/or following the instructions/
information described in this publication. Since the physical activities
described in this book, which involve, for example, kicks and heavy
throws, may be too strenuous in nature for some readers to engage in
safely, it is essential that a doctor be consulted prior to undertaking
training.

Throughout this book 'he', 'him' and 'his' have been used as neutral
pronouns and as such refer to both males and females.

Typeset by Jean Cussons Typesetting, Diss, Norfolk

Printed and bound in Great Britain by Biddles, King's Lynn

Contents

Introduction

First of all I will no doubt have to explain the title of the book, *Just Ju-Jitsu* (i.e., politics not included). My reasons for this title relate to my personal outlook on martial arts as a whole. Far too much is often made of 'this association (or style) is better than that one' or 'that grade doesn't count because it's not from our association'. I have heard these expressions, and ones like them, for my entire martial arts career and my response is much the same as that of my old *sensei* (teacher), which is to have nothing to do with such silliness. When all is said and done we train to better ourselves within our chosen martial art and not to be acceptable to a committee. For this reason I have not made reference to styles or associations within this book, just ju-jitsu.

The book is intended to be a general guide to *a* syllabus for ju-jitsu and not *the* syllabus; my main reason for starting it was to satisfy my own students' desires for a reference work on paper. The information in this book is meant to be dissected and used, or discarded as seems best to the individual reading it. The main aim I have is that everyone reading this book will find something in it to take away with them. Whether that be one technique or the entire syllabus matters not, only that the book has been of some use.

Within the book we will not only examine a basic syllabus from white belt to first *dan* (the first of the teaching grades) but also look at other areas surrounding the syllabus in more detail. These will range from body weapons, which form part of the art from the beginning, to weapon work, which normally comes later on. My reason for including chapters on these areas is to show the diversity of ju-jitsu as an art; each chapter is merely an introduction to that area as books can (and have) been written on those areas alone.

One final note: regardless of the syllabus you train by always remember that it is only the basic skeleton of *your* martial art. It forms a basis and, like a body, you need a strong skeleton to build upon. Also like a body the skeleton on its own is not of much use: it needs muscle, skin, organs, blood and much more just to function. The purpose of this book, and any syllabus, is to provide the skeleton. It is up to you to provide the rest, this is why no two people's expression of their martial art should be identical: similar maybe, but not identical. Just as everyone is an individual so should everyone's martial art be individual to them.

Enjoy the book and enjoy your art.

1 Basics

1. Etiquette

I have started with etiquette for two main reasons: the first is the importance of mutual respect within any martial art; the second is that unfortunately this is the area of least interest for most martial artists so I'll get it out of the way quickly so don't worry.

Shown here are the standing bow (*tachirei*) and kneeling bow (*zarei*). The bow in *ju-jitsu* is not a sign of subservience but is instead a sign of respect, either to one's *sensei*, to one's partner or to the *dojo* (training hall, literally 'the hall of the way'). On leaving the mat area or the *dojo* itself the *ju-jitsuka* (student) should always turn and perform a standing bow facing inwards. Likewise when entering the *dojo*, or when requesting permission from the sensei to walk onto the mat, a *tachirei* should be performed.

Both *tachirei* and *zarei* are performed at the beginning and end of a training session with the students facing the *sensei*. It is usual at such times for the *sensei* in charge of the mat to call for these bows, merely saying the word *rei*. Either *tachirei* or *zarei* (whichever is the most appropriate) is also performed to one's partner (*uke*) at the beginning and end of each section of training and to one's *sensei* after instruction (whether to the class as a whole or to individuals).

Etiquette is just as important for the *sensei* as for the students. The *sensei* whose *dojo* it is always remains in control of the *dojo* even when the class is being taken by another *sensei*. Any visiting *sensei* (other

Standing bow (*tachirei*).

Kneeling bow (*zarei*).

than the *dojo sensei*'s regular *sensei*) will act at all times as guests and defer to the *dojo sensei*, even if they are of a higher grade. If the *dojo sensei* has allowed another *sensei* (possibly one of his students) to start a lesson then that *sensei* remains in charge of that session until such time as the *dojo sensei* decides to take over the class or the starting *sensei* decides to hand the class over to another. Any *sensei* joining the class after the start would therefore either assist or train in their own right. It would be a breach of etiquette for any *sensei* (other than the *dojo*'s regular *sensei*) to take over a class uninvited once it has begun, regardless of their grade.

To an observer all these rules must seem, at best, quaint but it should be remembered that this is based on a martial tradition dating back to the ninth century and possibly earlier. Historically a failure to abide by these rules would result in death. Today a breach in etiquette would not necessarily be resolved so bloodily but failing to respect one's teacher, partner,

Basic short fighting stance.

environment and the potential lethality of the art could still result in serious injury or death: ju-jitsu is still a deadly art.

2. Basic Stance

Shown is the basic short fighting stance. This stance is formed by first standing with the feet shoulder width apart, moving the left foot forward by the same distance then turning the feet to point to the right by about forty-five degrees. This is basically how the stance is formed but each practitioner will need to adjust their feet within this basis until they are in a comfortable position. The hands are positioned as shown above with the left hand leading.

As with everything else in ju-jitsu this is not cast in stone. Practitioners must learn to judge for themselves whether to be in the above stance, a left-handed stance or something completely different. This is a basis from which to learn, a foundation, but in reality you would not necessarily be able to (or in some cases be advised to) stick rigidly to one stance. Ju-jitsu is about using the practitioner's own strengths and building upon them, and this means that each practitioner needs to be free to use or discard techniques which are not effective *for them*. No one technique works for everyone or on everyone; the art comes in learning oneself and learning to use the most effective technique.

As a student or an instructor it is very important to remember that just because a technique does not work for you that is not necessarily a good reason to discard it. Anyone having achieved, or seeking to achieve, their *dan* grade must accept the responsibility to learn and pass on as much as they can whether it works well for them or not. The reason for this is as I have already said: *everyone is different!* The technique that you dislike the most could turn

Side break-fall.

Four-point landing.

out to be one of your student's favourites. It is a *sensei*'s responsibility to give their students as broad a choice as possible.

It is a great mistake for any instructor to try and produce a class of unthinking robots who can perform all of their allotted techniques to a preordained minimum standard. Each student is an individual with both strengths and weaknesses and needs to be treated as such. A skilful *sensei* does not try to mould the student into their own image but instead finds the shape within the individual and does what is needed to bring this out.

3. Break-Falls

The most basic, and most used, break-fall is the side break-fall. The landing position is on one side (shown here) with that side's arm stretched out at a forty-five degree angle to the body, palm down. As someone progresses within the art they will come to realize that it is not the arm which is performing the break-fall but the whole body. The next picture shows the landing position for the 'four-flaps' (to northerners) or 'four-points' (to southerners) break-fall. This position is reached from a roll (either on the floor or in mid-air) and seeks to

keep the vulnerable back off the floor using both arms (again palms down) and both feet.

Next we have the rolling break-fall. Done from the left- or right-hand side this is again a way of shaping the whole body to minimize the impact with the floor (the floor is bigger and harder than you and it will hurt if you get it wrong!). Normally if the roll is being performed right-handed then the right foot is forward and vice versa. This is not an arbitrary decision by any means, most throws that need the rolling break-fall to fall from take the person being thrown over the lead leg, pulling forward on the same arm (thus putting the person in this right-arm right-leg position whether they like it or not). The arm is used as a guide and not as a support. When rolling the main point of contact on the back runs diagonally and the student needs to continue the roll and come up onto their feet. With practise the student should be able to come up in whatever orientation they wish, facing away from the attacker if they intend to run or facing towards them if they intend to fight (or cannot run). If they come up to face the attacker they should be in a fighting stance. About halfway through the roll the

9

Rolling break-fall (i).

Rolling break-fall (ii).

Rolling break-fall (iii).

Front break-fall.

non-lead arm slaps the floor (as for the side break-fall).

Shown is the front break-fall, this is used in similar circumstances to the rolling break-fall but where the student cannot roll (either because of the throw itself or due to limited space). With this break-fall the student lands on the balls of their feet and their forearms, and these are the only parts of the body to touch the floor. It is also a good idea with this break-fall to turn your head to one side: otherwise if your arms give way the next thing to hit the floor is your nose.

Although there are many different break-falls I have just given a brief description of the main ones. The reason for the brevity is because if you are already a student you will know them; if you are not already a student these would be the first thing you would be taught and they are fairly universal.

4. Balance and Handedness

An important thing to mention here before you read the rest of the book is that all of these techniques are practised left- and right-handed, from left- and right-hand attacks. Most of the time I will describe them right-handed, for ease of description. To do the technique on the opposite side just swap left for right and right for left.

The other area that will not be mentioned in every technique is balance. Balance is all-important in combat of every type: if you manage to keep yours and your opponent loses theirs then you've won. In each throw it is necessary to take your opponent off balance in the direction you wish to throw them. For example in the hip throw (*see* Chapter 5) it is necessary to bring your opponent forwards as you step in to perform the throw. The best way to imagine the balance point is as a Union Jack on top of your opponent's head: a cross and two diagonal lines. In very basic terms we have forwards, backwards, left, right, then the four diagonal combinations (left-backwards and so on).

5. *Tori* and *Uke*

One final point to mention: throughout this book I will refer to *tori* and *uke*, this is not for any archaic reason but a practical one, as it is easier to write and understand than the alternatives. In combat terms *tori* is you and *uke* is your attacker. In training terms *uke* is usually the aggressor and *tori* is the one performing the technique.

2 Body Weapons

Introduction

With ju-jitsu we use the entire body as a weapon. Even when we pick up a *katana* (sword) or *bo* (staff) we are still using the body as a weapon, they are merely an extension of that body. These 'additions' extend our range and increase the effectiveness of our techniques but do not in themselves alter the way we use our body.

In this chapter we will be having a brief look at a few of the strikes commonly used in ju-jitsu: these being the punch; the knife hand; the bottom fist; the ridge hand; the elbow and a few others.

With all strikes the main thing to remember is whatever force you are seeking to impart into your opponent you receive as well. This is basic physics, action and reaction; if you punch someone your fist will feel the same energy as the body. For this reason we train and condition the main striking areas to be able to sustain this impact.

Following on from this it must be realized that the energy has to go somewhere. If you punch something and it moves back, part of the energy is being dissipated to cause the movement. Likewise if you break something with a strike, part of the energy goes into that break. You can see a good example of this when someone tries to break wooden boards. If the boards break then no problem, but if they do not the force that would have gone into the break goes back into the fist. For this reason you will find that, for the same power of strike, hitting a board that breaks hurts a great deal less than hitting one that does not!

This dissipation of energy can work for us or against us, and it is experience that leads us to adjust our technique to best capitalize on this. For example, if you are doing a nerve strike to a 'soft' target area (*see* Appendix) any movement of the target away from you will reduce the effectiveness of the strike. Keeping the target from moving increases the strike effect but also the energy going back into the striking weapon, but since this is a soft target this does not cause much of a problem. Again if striking to a bone (a 'hard' target) you need the energy to be dissipated in a way most useful to you, most often this will be by the breaking of the bone rather than by motion.

An aspect of this dissipation of energy also occurs if the attacking 'weapon' (whether body or other) is drawn back too quickly. This has the effect of absorbing some of the energy of the blow in the action of drawing back; bouncing off the target this reduces the effect of the strike. To ensure that all of the kinetic energy is transferred through to the target the strike needs to stay on the target area for a fraction of a second after the blow has stopped moving. Meaning that you need to use more energy to draw the weapon back. The strikes should be aiming for a point a few inches past the point of impact anyway but there will normally be a point where the weapon stops moving. This principle is used very effectively in baton strikes to large muscle masses (such as the thigh) and the technical term for the physiological effect is called the 'fluid shock wave effect'. Don't worry about remembering the physics or the name, just remember and use the principle.

Another way to reduce the chance of injury to yourself is to choose the strike for the target properly and perform the strike correctly. An example of this is a normal punch: when done as described you are aligning the bones to minimize the *danger* to the weak points (the various joints in fingers and wrist).

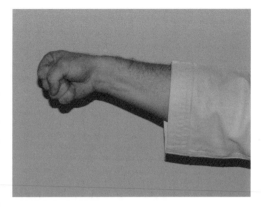

Normal fist (i).

1. Hands

A. Normal Fist
The clenched fist should curl the fingers into the meat of the palm pulling the bottom two knuckles inwards slightly. The thumb rests at the side of the fingers and the top two knuckles are tilted forward so that they are directly in-line with the radius bone of the forearm (the one next to the thumb). When looking from the top of the hand the hand should likewise be directly in-line with the arm. These factors take out the points of weakness: the finger joints, the lower two metacarpals and the wrist.

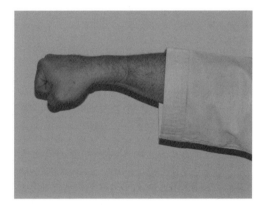

Normal fist (ii).

With all of these punches it is necessary to turn the upper body into the punch. For a right punch the body is rotating anticlockwise and for a left punch clockwise.

Jab
The jab from a fighting stance involves using the lead fist. The punch is short and straight to the target area. For all punches remember not to tense up until the point of impact and keep the attacking arm slightly bent (as a shock-absorber).

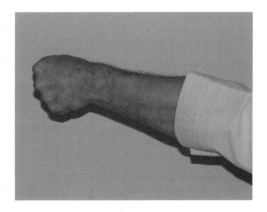

Normal fist (iii).

Jab.

Straight punch.

Hook.

Uppercut.

Straight

Sometimes called a cross punch. This uses the fist of the rear hand in a straight punch. This has greater power than the jab but is slightly slower. The reason for this is that it has further to go, making it easier to build up the power but giving it further to travel (another reason for the back hand being more powerful is that most people lead with their weak hand and therefore the back hand is the strongest).

Hook

From the left or right this punch uses a curving path to attack the side of the target.

Uppercut

This uses a curving path, as for the hook, but is doing so from underneath.

Lunge Punch

For this punch you are using the rear hand for the punch but as part of the punch you are stepping forward with the back leg. The motion of the two needs to be simultaneous so that the punch lands at the same time as the leg stops moving. So with

Lunge punch.

Backfist.

Bottom fist (forehand).

Bottom fist (backhand).

Bottom fist (downwards).

the example here the student has started with his right leg forwards, and has stepped forward with his left leg and brought his left punch in.

Backfist

Whereas the hook punch uses a fore-handed curved path the backfist uses a backhanded curved path. The aim is still to use the top two knuckles to strike but this time it is the back of the fist, not the front edge. Although this does not use the top two knuckles in the same way as the other punches above it does use the normal fist position, hence its inclusion here.

B. Bottom Fist

Also called the hammer fist, this strike uses the tough pad at the bottom of a clenched fist (by the little finger). By its nature it uses a curved path to reach its target. Shown here we have the forehanded hori-zontal, the backhanded horizontal and the vertical.

C. Leopard Punch

This strike involves bending the fingers at the second knuckle rather than at the top (first) knuckle, as with a normal fist. The first phalanges (finger bones) of each fin-ger should be in-line with the metacarpals

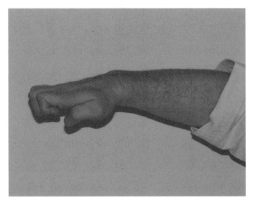

Leopard punch (formation).

Leopard punch (in use).

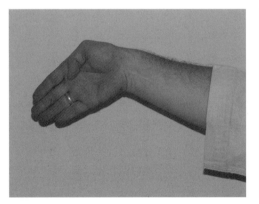

Ridge hand (formation).

Ridge hand (in use).

and the forearm; any bend introduces a weak point. This punch is used for 'soft' and 'semi-hard' target areas, in particular areas that require deep penetration (as shown here for the throat). The leopard punch is used as a straight punch, with no curve in its trajectory.

D. Ridge Hand

The ridge hand uses the bony projection on the wrist, just above the thumb. As you can see here the thumb is pulled underneath and the hand is rotated (in the plane of the palm) so that the straight fingers are rotated towards the little finger, exposing as much of the bony projection as possible. To bring this body weapon to bear the student normally uses a curved path. Shown here the path would be horizontal, anti-clockwise and the target is *uke*'s neck.

E. Knife Hand

To form the knife hand the little finger is brought inside the ring finger slightly, the thumb is brought into the palm and the hand is then curved slightly. The striking area for the knife hand is the pad of muscle that runs along the edge of the hand from

Knife hand (formation).

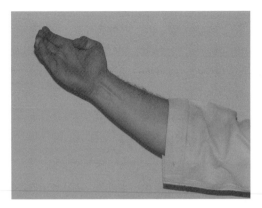

Knife hand (forehand).

Knife hand (backhand).

Knife hand (straight).

the base of the little finger to the wrist. Folding the little finger in and curving the hand should help you to tense up this muscle, but this will take training.

There are three main ways of using the knife hand. The first is the regular forehand style. Although you will, with practise, be able to shorten the distance your knife hand needs to travel to be effective I will describe it here at full range so that your initial practise will give you the proper 'feel' for the correct motion. The attacking hand is drawn back to the ear on the same side, with the elbow high behind

and the striking area (the little finger edge) facing upwards. To strike there are a couple of different rotations that need to happen simultaneously. The first is the striking hand itself; it needs to rotate from its starting position so that it ends up at right angles to the target area. In the picture shown the striking area of the hand will have gone through 270 degrees (three-quarters of a circle) clockwise, from pointing up to pointing horizontally to the left. This rotation should only finish at the point of impact and not before. The second rotation is the anticlockwise rotation

17

of *tori*'s hips. As *tori* is doing these two rotations his arm is extending out to bring the knife hand into the target area. The reason for the rotation in the hips is the same as for all of these strikes; it allows *tori* to put the power of his body into the strike and not just his arms. The rotation of *tori*'s hand (as opposed to starting with the striking area in the orientation needed for the strike) is to increase the effectiveness at the target area. The rotation has the effect of moving muscle out of the way of the strike (in a similar way a sawing motion with a knife blade normally cuts deeper than merely pressing the blade down). It also encourages the body to leave the strike in place for a fraction of a second (using the fluid shock wave effect discussed at the beginning of the chapter).

The second main style of knife hand is the backhanded one. Again I will describe the full path. This time the attacking arm comes across the front of *tori*'s body so that the attacking hand is level with the opposite ear, striking edge downwards. From here there are again the two separate rotations to be combined with the extension of the arm to the target. For the example shown here *tori*'s attacking hand rotates through ninety degrees (from downwards to horizontal and to the left) in a clockwise direction as the body twists anticlockwise.

The third type is the straight knife hand. This is different from the other knife hands in that it follows a straight path rather than a curved one. Also, although the body rotates (as it should for any strike including 'straight' strikes) the rotation of the striking area is in a different plane. The striking hand starts in the position for a normal fighting stance. The knife hand is formed (without the tension at this stage) and the fingers will point towards *uke*, thumb uppermost. The attacking arm does not rotate and its motion is straight at the target area. The attacking hand rotates only in the vertical plane, with the little finger rotating upwards so that at the point of impact the fingers are pointing upwards. Although similar to the palm heel strike you can see that the hand strikes edge-on rather than using the heel, this reduces the striking surface area thus increasing the pressure applied to the target.

F. Palm Heel

The palm heel is an extremely powerful weapon. The striking area is the tough pad running across the base of the hand just above the wrist. To bring this striking area to bear the fingers are pointed upwards, at right angles to the forearm. The thumb is locked in to the side of the fingers to keep it out of trouble and some people like to fold their fingers at the top so they are not too exposed (as shown here). This weapon can be used either straight or curved; I have shown a few examples here.

First we have a palm heel being used vertically. For this strike the attacking arm is kept bent and the curved rotation is brought in by the shoulder (and the hips of course).

Second we have an example of a curved palm heel being used horizontally. For this strike the attacking arm is straightening itself as the hips rotate. This combines a curved path caused by the hip rotation (and some of the arm motion) and a straight path caused by the arm. For those of you mathematically inclined the body describes a circle and at the point of your choosing the arm breaks off at a tangent, the rotational momentum adding to the force of the blow. For those of you not so inclined it is the same as swinging a weight on a string around your head, then choosing the point of release at which point the weight travels in a straight direction.

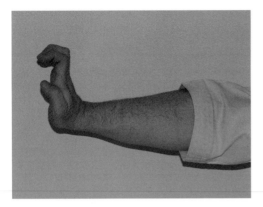

Palm heel (formation).

Palm heel (vertical).

Palm heel (horizontal).

Palm heel (straight).

The third palm heel is the straight palm heel. The body twists and the attacking arm extends straight out to the target, fingers pointing up.

G. Fingers

This category of strikes involves the use of one or more extended fingers. While I have known people develop their finger strikes to the point where they can poke holes in Coke cans I would still advise that these are used for the 'soft' and 'semi-hard' target areas and not the 'hard' targets. These are used in a straight fashion, thrusting rather than cutting.

Single Finger
Shown here reinforced against the folded fingers.

Double Finger
Here the first and second fingers are used and the others drawn fully out of the way. The second finger is resting on top of the first finger and tensed to reinforce the fingers.

Spear Hand
(Again you can see the comparison to a thrusting weapon.) For this strike the fingers are straight and directly in-line with

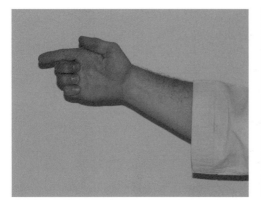

Single finger.

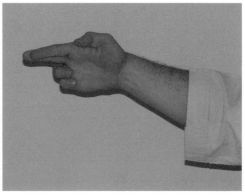

Double finger.

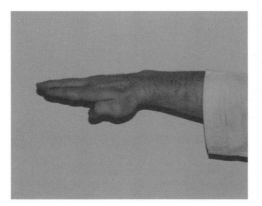

Spear hand (side).

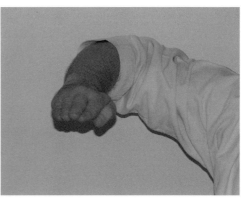

Spear hand (end view).

Spear hand (in use).

the body of the hand and the forearm. The first finger and the little finger are slipped slightly under the fingers next to them for added strength. Looking at the fingers head-on the fingers appear to form a curve (stronger than the straight line).

H. Thumbs

Shown here, the thumb when used for a strike extends over the top of the fist. As well as a strike it is useful for attacking nerve points.

I. Knuckles

The main knuckle strikes shown here are

20

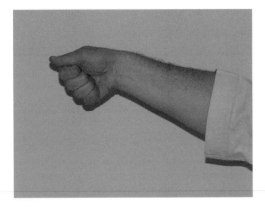

Thumb (formation).

Thumb (in use).

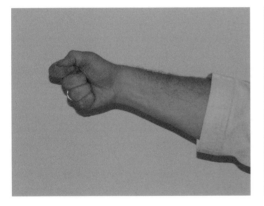

Top knuckle.

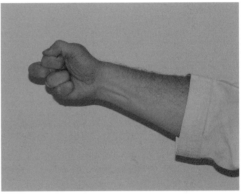

Second knuckle.

the first knuckle and the second knuckle. In both cases the knuckle extends from the fist for added strength. Examples can be seen being used to attack the eyes in Chapter 12. In this third example we see the top knuckle being used to attack (strike or direct pressure) the nerves at the brachial plexus origin.

2. Elbows

The elbows are a body weapon that can be used to impart a huge amount of force. The arm is bent so that the forearm is tight against the bicep, thus the first point of

Knuckle against nerve.

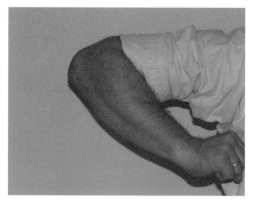

Elbow (formation).

Elbow (downwards).

Elbow (backwards).

Elbow (upwards).

Elbow (forehand).

Elbow (backhand).

weakness is the shoulder. By doing this we are removing all of the weak points from the hand, wrist and elbow joint. The elbow can be used from virtually any direction but we are just going to look at four main ones here. The four directions are up, down, left and right; from these any of the other directions can be worked out.

The first direction shown here does not appear to link into these four: backwards. This is not true. The backwards elbow is the continuation of the downwards elbow. For the downward strike the elbow starts level with the shoulder, with the body twisted so that that shoulder is pushed forward. From there the elbow comes down and back, rotating about the shoulder; at the same time the shoulder (the forward shoulder, the same side as the elbow being used) moves backwards. If the target is in front then added force can be applied to the strike by bending your knees and therefore adding your body weight to the force of the blow.

The second direction shown here is in the same plane but upwards. This time the elbow starts behind *tori*, so that the fist of that arm is level with *tori*'s chest. The upper body is twisted clockwise so that the shoulder of the elbow to be used is pulled back. The elbow is rotated upwards, rotating about the shoulder, and the upper body twisted anticlockwise bringing the shoulder forward.

For the third example here we are looking at the horizontal forehanded elbow. The elbow is level with the shoulder and the shoulder is drawn back. For best effect the upper arm of the elbow being used stays in the same plane as the chest. In order to keep the elbow at this level *tori* needs to bend his knees to bring the elbow to the right height for the target. *Tori* then steps in to *uke* and at the same time brings his elbow forward by twisting his upper

body back, bringing the attacking shoulder forward.

The backhand horizontal elbow is shown here for the right elbow. *Tori* twists his upper body anticlockwise and brings his elbow in front of *uke* (just under the chin). *Tori* then steps in to *uke* and twists his upper body clockwise, at the same time extending his elbow straight out to the side.

3. Head

The head is an area of the body that I don't particularly like using (I'm very attached to the contents and don't want them damaged!) but there are circumstances where the head is the most appropriate weapon to be used (usually when

Head (front (i)).

Head (front (ii)).

Head (backwards).

being held). There is nothing subtle about the use of the head; it just requires a sharp movement either forwards or backwards. The main thing to be aware of with using the head is what area of the head to use and which areas to aim for. For the front head-butt the striking area is the top of the forehead. For the backwards head strike the striking area is the corresponding area on the back of the head (don't use the area of the back of the head that is any lower than this, as you would be in *dan*ger of injuring the medulla oblongata (the nobbly bit at the base of the skull). The target area in both cases shown is the nose.

3 Blocks and Parries

1. Inside Forearm Parry

This is the most commonly used parry and many aspects of it are used in the other parries described. The part of the arm that makes contact with the attacking strike is halfway down the inside of the forearm. Taking the left arm parry shown here we can see that the left arm is bent and the hand has been turned anticlockwise (thumb forward, little finger back) so that the back of the hand is facing back towards *tori*. This means that the attacking strike will impact the arm on the muscle of the forearm rather than the bone, allowing the muscle to act as a shock-absorber. The point of *uke* that is parried here is also halfway down the forearm; blocking higher can allow the rest of the limb to swing around and still hit. This only describes

the motion of the arm, and as with all parries and blocks this is only part of the story. With the ordinary inside forearm parry the parrying arm is moving up and to the left (twisting as described) and at the same time *tori* is moving his head to the right. This moves the target for the strike out of the strike's path in case the parry fails. Because the head is moved away there is no need to fully arrest the motion of *uke*'s strike, just redirect it slightly and keep it moving forward (such forward momentum being used to take *uke* off balance).

The second of the inside forearm parries involves the same arm movement but intercepts the strike far earlier before it has built up any real momentum. For this *tori* extends their front foot (left shown here)

Inside forearm parry (static).

Inside forearm parry (stepping in).

25

forwards and slightly to the left of *uke*'s right foot while bringing their left arm up to parry. The movement has to be done as soon as *uke* starts to move so that *uke*'s attacking arm is still very near its starting point. Because *tori* is moving his body weight forward and connecting with *uke*'s arm before he can commit his own weight forward it has the effect of taking *uke* off balance to the rear (and, shown here, to *tori*'s right). So both parries, when done correctly, can take *uke* off balance before any technique is attempted.

2. Outside Forearm Parry

The outside forearm parry shares many characteristics with section one, [above]. It redirects the blow rather than stopping it and as such throws *uke* off balance. It can be done using the leading arm or the trailing arm (with a normal left short fighting stance the leading arm is the left). The parry is the same for both only the arm changes. Shown here we have the leading arm parry: *tori* steps forward and to the left with his left leg slightly bent (aligned

roughly at a forty-five degree angle), and at the same time brings his left arm up and parries the outside of *uke*'s forearm. As well as being done with either arm from the same stance it can be done stepping with either foot; try all the combinations.

When practising both the inside and outside forearm parries you will find that it does not make any difference which arm *uke* strikes with. If you are starting to do a left inside forearm parry (expecting a right punch to the face) and *uke* attacks with a left punch you will find (if you have done it right) that the parry still works but it now appears to be an outside parry!

3. Downward Inside Forearm Parry

Shown here we can see that *tori* brings his left arm down and outwards. As before the arm is twisting outwards, to present the forearm muscle as the parrying surface, and connects with *uke* halfway down his forearm. As the arm goes down *tori* twists his body slightly clockwise and backwards (avoidance again).

Outside forearm parry.

Downward inside forearm parry.

Downward outside forearm parry.

Upward rising block.

4. Downward Outside Forearm Parry

Here *tori* steps forward at a forty-five degree angle with his left foot and swings his left forearm down to parry *uke*'s arm. The movement of the parrying arm should again bring the muscle in as the parrying surface and *tori* should have the feeling of the elbow going slightly faster than the hand so that at the point of parry the elbow is directly below the hand. At the same time the left arm is moving to parry the right leg is also moving. This foot movement is far subtler and just involves *tori* moving their trailing right foot a little to the left so that it is in-line with their front foot. This has two effects: the first is that this movement means once *tori* has finished moving his body to parry he will still be in stance facing *uke* (but off to one side of *uke* and out of *uke*'s fighting arc); it also means that the target is no longer in the path of *uke*'s strike, which is always a good thing!

5. Upward Rising Block

Here we come to a true block, meaning

that we are arresting the motion of *uke*'s strike. *Uke* is attacking with a downward strike to *tori*'s head and *tori* moves in to block. For this block to be effective *tori* needs to intercept the strike before it has time to build up momentum (you will notice a theme here). *Tori* moves forward slightly with their left foot and brings their left arm up above their head so that the forearm is horizontal. As before the forearm rotates as it moves in to block, to present the muscle to the attacking strike. For this block it is done by rotating the palm outwards, which brings the little finger up and the thumb down.

6. Cross Block (static and stepping back)

The cross block shown here is used to arrest the movement of a punch to the upper body or head. The upper body movement is identical whether it is done stepping back or statically, only the foot movement changes.

The most commonly used cross block is done from a left short fighting stance (left leg forwards); it involves stepping back

27

Cross block (stepping back).

Cross block (static).

with the left leg and is done in response to a lunge punch (*see* Chapter 2). *Tori* steps back with the left leg and turns his body anticlockwise about ninety degrees (from a forty-five degree stance, left leg forward, to a forty-five degree stance, right leg forward). In doing this *tori*'s right arm will naturally swing forwards and to the left. *Tori* uses this motion and adds to it, bringing his forearm (muscle first) in to block *uke*'s forearm (as with section four, (above), *tori*'s elbow should be moving slightly faster than his hand so that at the point of impact the elbow is directly below the hand).

The static cross block has exactly the same arm movements but here *tori* already has the same leg forward as the blocking arm, for a right cross block this means that they are in a right stance (right foot forward). For this block *tori*'s body moves anticlockwise from forty-five to ninety degrees but his arm movement remains the same as above. Because of the reduced body movement this static block is not quite as strong as the stepping-back cross block but the situations in which it is used will normally involve strikes which are not as strong: it is shown here against a right cross punch (*see* Chapter 2) which, while faster than the lunge punch, is not quite as powerful.

7. Palm Heel Blocks

Palm heel blocks and parries are slightly different than the earlier blocks and parries. This is because when done correctly they are not only a defence but also a potentially damaging strike at the same time. Three palm heel blocks are shown in the purple belt syllabus (*see* Chapter 11) so I won't repeat myself here. The reason they are shown at a higher level is not for the safety of the practitioner but their partner. The potential damage requires a great deal of control in training which you should have obtained in order to reach that grade.

X block (initial block).

X block (locking of wrist).

8. X Block

This can be done to defend against upwards strikes to the groin or (as shown here) downward strikes to the head. *Tori* brings both arms up twisting them both as if they were doing the upward rising block described earlier. The only difference here is that both arms are at a forty-five degree angle to the vertical and they cross at the wrist. At the point they cross it is usually best to have the front arm of the cross (the one nearest to *uke*) on the same side as *tori*'s front foot. Once the attack makes contact at the centre of the crossed wrists *tori* twists his hands further, as if trying to get their little fingers to meet, thus trapping *uke*'s arm and giving *tori* control.

4 Kicks

I am using this general title to go through the basic strikes in ju-jitsu using the legs; the same basic principles of physics discussed in Chapter 2 apply here. The main kicks within ju-jitsu are: front snap kicks, crescent kicks, side thrust kicks, side snap kicks, roundhouse kicks, spinning back kicks and knee strikes. There are a large number of foot and leg strikes described within this book that do not fall into these categories and that is because the kicks described here are those that can be used offensively. You may also have noticed that I have not included 'flying kicks'. Most kicks can be altered to become flying kicks but if you are interested in these it is best to speak to an individual *sensei*. My personal opinion is that they should only ever be used where an obstacle needs to be cleared to allow escape and there is an opponent on the other side of the obstacle. As I have said before this is only an opinion, it is not gospel, and if you are interested you should research the subject.

1. Front Snap Kicks

These are the first kicks taught, as they are the least technically demanding. Do not however get hung up on their simplicity; some of the most effective and useful things in the world are simple.

Shown here we have *tori* in a left short fighting stance (basic fighting stance). From this stance the left front snap kick is the faster snap kick and right front snap kick is the more powerful. For the left front snap kick *tori* leans his weight back onto

Left front snap kick (i).

Left front snap kick (ii).

Right front snap kick (i).

Right front snap kick (ii).

his right leg, so that his centre of balance is over it, and bends the left leg so that his left foot is level with his right knee. *Tori* then pushes the left foot out sharply towards the target, and as described in previous chapters the strike should be aimed several inches beyond target. Once the target has been struck *tori* reverses the above motion, bringing the left leg back horizontally until it is bent at the knee again. *Tori* then places his foot down and returns his balance back into the fighting stance. The easiest way to practise this sequence at first is to have some obstacle directly in front of your left knee that is knee-high. It is also important to remember that the striking area for these two kicks are either the pad of the bottom of the foot or the heel (depending on how flexible your feet are), so the toes need to be pulled back away from the target. For these two kicks the kicking foot should always be toes up and heel down, not angled.

For the right front snap kick the procedure is the same: the weight is transferred to the non-kicking foot (left) and the right foot is raised to knee height. The right foot is thrust out at the target then returned to knee height and placed back where it started.

2. Crescent Kick

The crescent kick in ju-jitsu is different from that described in other martial arts but when all is said and done it is merely a name.

In ju-jitsu the crescent kick is to the right (back foot) snap kick what the lunge punch is to the cross punch. It is performed in much the same way as the snap kick, the differences being in the balance and finish.

The balance is transferred to the front foot and the right foot brought up to knee height as with the snap kick. From here *tori* thrusts out at the target with the back foot but unlike the snap kick *tori* puts all of his body weight forward and powers the foot through the target. Once through the target *tori*'s foot comes down leaving him

Crescent kick (i).

Crescent kick (ii).

in a reversed stance (if he started in a left-foot-forward stance he should finish right-foot-forward and vice versa). I have shown the start and finish here, the middle is the same as for the right front snap kick.

3. Side Thrust Kicks

These powerful kicks can be performed using the front or rear foot, and although the strike itself is the same the method of achieving it differs somewhat.

Shown here we have a front-foot side thrust kick performed from a right stance. *Tori* turns his body slightly so that he is fully side-on to the target then brings his left (back) foot forwards so that it finishes just in front of the right foot, side-on to the target (the moving leg passes behind the stationary one). He then draws the right foot up to knee height and thrusts out at the target. Note that the striking area is the heel and that the foot is kept horizontal throughout the kick (possibly with the toes pulled back and slightly down if your flexibility will allow). As with the crescent kick,

the kicking foot goes through the target and remains forward.

For the back-foot version (shown again from a right stance) *tori* brings his left (back) foot up in the same way as for a snap kick. From this position *tori* pivots on his right (front) foot so that it is horizontal to the target, pivoting his body so that it is side-on to the target. *Tori* then thrusts out at the target. As mentioned for the front-foot version the striking foot remains horizontal (toes back and slightly down) but with this version after the thrust through *uke tori* has the option of leaving the foot forward (reversed stance) or reversing the kick back to the starting position. It is important to remember to put the kick through the target in both cases (otherwise you will be doing a side snap kick, described opposite).

Remember not to get too hung up on front and back. If you are facing one direction in left stance and an opponent approaches from your right a simple turn of the upper body means that you are now facing that opponent in a right stance. Be

Side thrust kick (front foot (i)).

Side thrust kick (front foot (ii)).

Side thrust kick (front foot (iii)).

Side thrust kick (back foot (i)).

Side thrust kick (back foot (ii)).

flexible and once you have the basics, don't be afraid to improvise.

4. Side Snap Kicks

As with the side thrust kicks these can be done with the front foot or the back foot.

For the front side snap kick the balance is shifted back and the left (front) foot is brought up to knee level (as for the left front snap kick). From here the foot is snapped out and at the same time *tori* twists his hips clockwise so that at the point of impact the striking foot and the body exactly resemble the side thrust kick with the foot horizontal. *Tori* then reverses the motion and brings them back into the left stance.

The rear side snap kick again starts like the rear front snap kick. The balance is placed onto the left foot and the right (rear) foot is brought up to knee level. From here *tori* thrusts the right foot out and pivots his body anticlockwise so that again at the point of impact the kick is the same as the side thrust kick. *Tori* then quickly reverses the motion and returns to his original stance.

Roundhouse kick (i).

Roundhouse kick (ii).

Roundhouse kick (iii).

The main differences between this and the side thrust kick are that with the side snap kick *tori* pivots to bring the side of the foot to bear during the last part of the kick, then quickly withdraws the foot. Consequently the side snap kick is faster but less powerful than the side thrust kick, which accounts for a different target area. Shown in Chapter 10 the side snap kick can be used against the knees which are a very mobile target (meaning the attack needs to be quick) but also a very vulnerable target in virtually anyone (thus requiring slightly less force to be effective than for some areas).

5. Roundhouse Kicks

These kicks are covered as part of several techniques so I am giving only a general description here.

Spinning back kick (i).

Spinning back kick (ii).

Spinning back kick (iii).

Spinning back kick (iv).

The roundhouse kick can be a very fast kick and is used in numerous ways. In its most basic form, shown here from a left stance, *tori* turns his left foot to point left and brings his balance over it. *Tori* then brings his right knee up to waist level and forwards while pivoting his upper body away from the raised leg: this has the effect of starting the body in an anticlockwise rotation. *Tori* uses this rotation to bring his right knee further forward and then pivots more allowing his lower right leg to straighten and swing anticlockwise. Control is important with this rotation;

if it is done too fast recovery is difficult. *Tori* has the choice of kicking through *uke* and finishing in a reversed stance or reversing the motion back to his original position.

The striking area for this kick is different depending on the target, the desired effect and the range. The main areas used are the top of the foot (with the toes pointing so that the top of the foot is in-line with the shin), the shin, the ball of the foot (specific targets and requires a great deal of flexibility) and the heel for the reversed roundhouse (*see* Chapter 9).

Knee strike (straight).

Knee strike (roundhouse).

Knee strike (upwards).

6. Spinning Back Kick

For the left kick (shown here) *tori* steps forward with the right foot then turns his body anticlockwise allowing him to look over his left shoulder at the target. *Tori* brings his right leg up so the foot is at knee level and thrusts it at the target. I have broken down the mechanics of the kick here but an important thing to remember with this kick is that from the initial step (here with the right) *tori* is in constant motion until their foot makes contact with *uke*. This means that the clockwise spinning motion adds to the force of the thrusting leg.

7. Knee Strikes

Knee strikes are extremely powerful but due to the striking area used are obviously limited in range. As with kicks they can be used straight (as for the front snap kick), in a roundhouse fashion or upwards. The main thing to remember with all knee strikes is to ensure that the knee is fully bent, this immobilizes your patella (kneecap) thus preventing any dislocation. The motion of the body is the same as that for the kick that follows the same pattern.

Knee strikes are described in various places through the book, most of the time as a weakener or distraction technique rather than as a means unto themselves. In close fighting they can be extremely effective (just look at your average *muay thai* fight!), so practise them well.

5 White Belt

All of the techniques are described, for simplicity's sake, as if done in a right-handed fashion. You should however practise both sides as much as possible. You will always find that you favour one side over another but, not always the same side for all techniques, and in actual combat you will not have the luxury of choice.

1. Hip Throw

As this is the first technique I will take a few lines to describe the basic block used here. Although we call it a block it is more accurately described as a parry since we use it to redirect rather than to stop. The arm is brought up from its ready position (basic fighting stance) and the fist is twisted outwards. At the same time you must move your head and shoulders in the other direction. Twisting the arm presents the forearm muscle as the blocking area and adds to the effectiveness of the parry. Moving the head ensures that even if the arm fails to parry the blow the head is no longer there to be hit (for more of a description *see* Chapter 3).

From this parry *tori* takes hold of *uke*'s right arm with his parrying arm and pulls *uke* forwards off balance and then steps forward placing his right foot next to the inside of *uke*'s right foot. Pivoting on the ball of the right foot *tori* brings his left foot into the position shown, placing his right arm around *uke*'s waist at the same time. Moving into this position *tori* must bend his knees to bring his hips below *uke*'s centre of gravity (usually the belt).

Tori then leans forward and straightens his legs. At the same time he needs to pull *uke* around with his left arm. In practice it is best to maintain the hold on *uke*'s right arm (left arm if the technique is being done left-handed) to make the break-fall easier.

2. Basic Front Grab Escapes

Where the grab is a strangle (as shown for the first technique) the chin is lowered and the shoulders raised, this takes the pressure off the strangle. In all cases *tori* raises his left hand, palm outwards, in order to protect the face.

(i) Once in the position described above *tori* steps back with his left foot and at the same time brings his right arm over *uke*'s arms in a wide arc finishing at *tori*'s left hip. The technique is then finished with a strike to the right hand side of *uke*'s face using a backfist (or an elbow if *uke* is too close). The backwards step must be accompanied with a twist of the body to the left and a shift of the weight towards the back (left) foot as shown in the photographs.

(ii) From a start position of being grabbed by both lapels *tori* guards his face with his left hand. *Tori* steps back on the left leg slightly, turning his hips anticlockwise, and

Hip throw (stepping in).   Hip throw (positioning feet).   Hip throw (throw).

Basic escape from a front grab (strangle protection).

Basic escape from a front grab (head-butt protection).

brings his right palm heel up between *uke*'s arms to strike the underneath of the chin (this on its own could solve the problem!). *Tori* then brings his right elbow down onto *uke*'s left arm, bending it. From here *tori* wraps his right arm around *uke*'s left (clockwise), keeping the elbow bent, and brings *uke*'s hand up towards his own face. If it has been done correctly *uke*'s left hand should be stuck in *tori*'s right armpit and *uke*'s left arm should be bent in an L-shape with the elbow up near his own chin.

Basic escape from a front grab ((i) a).

Basic escape from a front grab ((i) b).

Basic escape from a
front grab ((ii) a).

Basic escape from a
front grab ((ii) b).

Basic escape from a
front grab ((ii) c).

Note: these two techniques are practised as if from either a strangle or from one of a variety of more commonplace attacks. The most obvious, shown in the second example, is where an attacker grabs your jacket in both hands to pull you into a head-butt.

This is the reason for the left-hand guard, to stop an intentional head-butt or, where *tori* strikes to the solar plexus or below, to stop an unintentional one (if you hit someone hard in the solar plexus they will normally bend forward!).

Body drop from a rear grab (weakening strike).

Body drop from a rear grab (throw position).

Body drop from a rear grab (throw).

3. Body Drop from a Rear Grab

For sections three and four if the grab is a basic strangle they are started with the same chin-down 'shrug' as for section two. For both techniques *tori* needs to step to his left and slightly backwards with his left foot only; doing this opens up *uke*'s chest as a target area.

For the body drop *tori* strikes to *uke*'s solar plexus using his right elbow. *Tori* then places his right arm around *uke*'s waist and grasps *uke*'s right arm with his left hand while at the same time extending his right leg so that it is in front of both of *uke*'s legs. *Tori* then pulls *uke* over his extended leg using both arms. Note that *tori*'s right foot and knee are facing directly away from *uke*; this is for *tori*'s safety if *uke* should fall onto that leg (in this position *tori*'s leg will bend, if the knee were pointing upwards his leg would break instead!) and also for increased effectiveness (see the body drop in Chapter 5 for a full description).

4. Shoulder Lock from a Rear Grab

In this technique *tori* again strikes with the right elbow to *uke*'s solar plexus but then follows up with a right backfist to the groin. *Tori* then turns ninety degrees to his right leaving his left foot where it is and stepping out with his right foot. He then places his right hand under *uke*'s left arm and onto the shoulder where it is joined by *tori*'s left hand. This should be made easier by the fact that the strikes will have had the quite natural effect of bending *uke*! The position this should leave you in is a shoulder lock, which is explained further below. Pivoting on the right foot and bringing the left foot around a quarter-turn to the left will help place *uke* fully in the lock.

Shoulder lock from a rear grab (secondary strike).

Shoulder lock from a rear grab (shoulder take).

5. Shoulder Lock

This technique is used for defending against a punch to the stomach with *tori* parrying the inside of *uke*'s forearm. In this instance *tori* needs to move his body slightly to his right while parrying with his left. Once they have parried *tori* can then strike with his right fist to *uke*'s solar plexus (this gives *uke* something to think about other than the lock you are about to perform on him!). *Tori*'s left arm slides up the inside of *uke*'s arm and his hand goes under the armpit to come to rest on *uke*'s right shoulder. *Tori* then places his right hand on top of his left and pivots on his left foot in a clockwise motion until he is facing the same way as *uke*, with his right foot behind his left. This should leave *uke* bent at the middle with his right arm vertical resting in the crook of *tori*'s left elbow. To apply the lock *uke*'s shoulder is pulled in to rest against *tori*'s hip and his

Shoulder lock from a rear grab (turn to apply the lock).

Shoulder lock (weakening strike).

Shoulder lock (hand placement).

Shoulder lock (turn to apply the lock).

arm is levered towards *tori*'s left ear. Some people find this technique more effective with *uke*'s arm resting on top of their shoulder rather than in the crook of their arm; try both and see which works best for you.

6. Straight-Arm Lock

This technique is performed as a defence against a punch to the stomach (shown from a right punch). *Tori* parries the outside of *uke*'s arm with his left forearm, elbow down and hand up. As *Tori* is parrying he needs to move his back foot (right in this case) to the left behind his left foot. This means that *uke*'s target (*tori*'s body!) is no longer in the path of his fist, thus even if *tori*'s parry fails to deflect *uke*'s blow he will still not get hit (important!). *Tori* then grabs *uke*'s right wrist with his right hand and turns the arm so that *uke*'s palm is facing upwards. He then strikes *uke*'s face with his left elbow. Depending on the relative size of *uke* and *tori* it may be necessary for *tori* to move in to *uke* with this strike (keeping the feet the same). *Tori* then circles *uke*'s right arm with his left so that *tori*'s hand comes as high up as possible on his own chest. *Tori* then squeezes with the left arm while pushing *uke*'s wrist downwards.

There are a couple of important things to remember with this technique. First, as with all locks this must always be done slowly and carefully (in training at any rate), releasing pressure when *uke* indicates that the lock is on. Second, always bring your opponent to your level. If they are taller than you use the initial strike to the face and the subsequent circling of *uke*'s right arm with your left in order to bring them down to you, do not reach up to their height.

Straight-arm lock (parry and grab).

Straight-arm lock (strike to face).

Straight-arm lock (apply lock).

7. Ankle Throw from the Ground

In a real-life situation this technique is done when you have ended up on the floor and must defend yourself from there. It is not a good idea to throw yourself to the floor in order to do the technique. It is normally practised from a push that causes you to fall to the floor. This is for two reasons: first just in case you are pushed and fall (something to avoid), and secondly to practise controlling your side break-falls (a good idea at this early stage in a student's training).

Ankle throw from prone (ankle hook).

On the floor *tori* lies on his side with the top leg (left in the picture) drawn up so that the knee covers the groin area. When *uke* steps forward *tori* hooks his bottom foot around the back of *uke*'s lead leg, at the ankle. *Tori* then strikes at *uke*'s knee with his top foot. To finish *tori* brings himself upright and delivers a kick to *uke*'s groin on the way up.

Note that in training you would gently push *uke*'s leg just above the knee, not strike it. Remember you want to be able to train with this person, not maim them (besides, it's their turn next!).

Ankle throw from prone (applying technique).

6 Yellow Belt

1. Body Drop

This is one of those techniques that (like the hip throw) I think of as a foundation technique. As such it is important to be completely comfortable with this throw (in the words of Musashi, 'you must study this well').

The throw is shown as a defence from a right punch to the face. *Tori* defends with a left inside forearm parry and takes hold of *uke*'s right hand with his left. *Tori* brings his right foot forward until it is just in front of *uke*'s left foot then pivots on his right bringing his left foot around until it is next to the right (work your way through all the lefts and rights and look at the picture, it will make sense). While moving into this position (both feet together by *uke*'s left foot, knees slightly bent and facing the same way as *uke*) *tori* needs to bring his right arm around *uke*'s waist. With the left leg bent *tori* extends his right leg out in front of *uke*'s legs. *Tori*'s right leg should be only slightly bent, the back of his knee touching *uke*'s right leg and the toes of the right foot should be pointing directly ahead (not to the right and definitely not upwards!). Once in this position *tori* completes the throw by pulling *uke*'s right arm across the front of his chest (*tori*'s) and aids this pull by bringing his right hand around to the front of his body (pulling *uke*'s body, which it has encircled, with it). While pulling *uke* over the outstretched right leg *tori* sharply straightens this leg, snapping it backwards onto *uke*'s right leg.

Body drop (initial foot movement).

Body drop (turn in).

Body drop (final leg position).

Body drop (throw).

Cross-arm lock (start position).

Cross-arm lock (face stamp).

2. Cross-Arm Lock from a Throw

This starts with a basic throw and ends with *uke* lying horizontal in front of *tori* and with *tori* having hold of *uke*'s right arm. *Tori* then takes hold of *uke*'s right hand with both of his. *Tori* does this by having both of his thumbs in the middle of the back of *uke*'s hand with *uke*'s palm facing away from them. *Tori* then pulls upwards so that *uke* is pulled off his back onto his side. *Tori* then kicks *uke* in the back with his right foot, just to the right of

Cross-arm lock (applying lock).

Ground defence against kicks ((i) a).

Ground defence against kicks ((i) b).

Ground defence against kicks ((i) c).

uke's upraised arm. *Tori* then stamps on *uke*'s face with his left foot so that the foot comes to rest in front of *uke*'s neck. *Tori* draws his left foot back so that it is tight against *uke*'s neck and then sits down as close to *uke* as possible. *Tori* then lies back pulling *uke*'s arm across the inside of one of their thighs with *uke*'s palm facing upwards. To apply the lock *tori* then raises his hips off the floor, thus using the powerful muscles of the leg rather than just the arms. To finish *tori* strikes *uke* to the sternum with his left heel then pushes him away with both feet and stands.

As with all techniques I have described this as it would be done against a real opponent, when practising you would obviously not perform the strikes fully.

3. Ground Defences Against Kicks

The starting position for these two techniques can be either lying on the left side or on the right. Both fists are in the clenched position covering the face with the backs of the hands facing *tori*. The top leg (the one furthest from the floor when lying on your side) is bent so that the knee is protecting the groin. The first of the two techniques is best used when *uke* kicks with the foot nearest to *tori*'s head and the second when *uke* kicks with the foot nearest to *tori*'s groin. In practice it is best to start with the kicks being aimed at *tori*'s upper chest.

(i) *Tori* blocks the incoming kick with both forearms. *Tori* then strikes the back of *uke*'s kicking knee with his uppermost arm then brings his uppermost leg up and behind *uke*'s kicking leg. *Tori* then twists as if rolling onto his back which brings *uke* to the floor, face down. To finish *tori* places the thinnest part of his lower leg (the same

Ground defence against kicks ((ii) a).

Ground defence against kicks ((ii) b).

Standing armlock ((i) a).

Standing armlock ((i) b).

leg that pushed *uke* to the ground) into the hollow at the back of *uke*'s kicking leg and then continues his roll towards *uke* bringing *uke*'s leg up in front of him. Once in this position the back of *uke*'s head is open for a strike as are his kidneys.

(ii) Here the block is the same as for the previous example but *tori* then wraps his right arm around the attacking leg and rolls in to *uke*'s leg to perform the sacrificing leg throw shown later in this chapter.

4. Standing Arm Locks

(i) This first lock, commonly called the figure-four armlock, starts (as do all techniques unless otherwise stated) in a short fighting stance. *Uke* strikes downwards to *tori*'s head, *tori* then blocks with a left upward rising block (*see* Chapter 3) and takes hold of *uke*'s right wrist with his blocking hand. *Tori* then steps in with his right foot and brings his right arm up and under *uke*'s right arm. This motion of the arm ends with a strike to the far side of *uke*'s elbow causing *uke*'s arm to bend. *Tori* uses this bend and, with his right arm behind *uke*'s upper arm, grabs hold of *uke*'s wrist. The lock is applied by *tori* lowering his right hand and raising his right elbow.

Standing armlock ((ii) a).

Standing armlock ((ii) b).

Standing armlock ((iii) a).

Standing armlock ((iii) b).

Standing armlock ((iii) c).

Standing armlock ((iii) d).

Sacrificing leg throw (initial take).

Sacrificing leg throw (final position with strike).

(ii) This technique starts from the same downwards strike by *uke* and the same upwards rising block from *tori*; *tori* again grabs *uke*'s right wrist with his left hand. This time *tori* strikes downwards onto the crook of *uke*'s right elbow with his right arm causing it to bend. *Tori* then takes his right arm over *uke*'s upper arm and behind *uke*'s forearm. In this position *tori* grabs his own left wrist in his right hand and applies the lock by lowering his left hand.

(iii) This move starts with *uke* attacking *tori*'s face (whether with a fist or a thrusting weapon). *Tori* moves forwards and to the left (at a forty-five degree angle) and parries the outside of *uke*'s arm with their right forearm. *Tori* then takes hold of *uke*'s wrist in his right hand and strikes *uke* to the face with a left palm heel strike. *Tori* then brings his left hand back sharply to strike the inside of *uke*'s elbow. The sudden bend in *uke*'s right arm is assisted by *tori* pushing *uke*'s hand (and whatever is in it) straight at *uke*'s face. *Tori* keeps his left arm in the crook of *uke*'s elbow and once *uke*'s hand reaches his own face *tori* moves it

behind *uke*'s forearm and grabs his other wrist. Continuing the motion of *uke*'s hand to behind his head then applies the lock.

5. Sacrificing Leg Throw

The term 'sacrificing' is used here to indicate that *tori* is sacrificing his standing position. *Uke* attacks with a punch to the face which *tori* blocks with a normal inside forearm parry. *Tori* then places his right knee on the floor next to *uke*'s lead leg facing at a right angle to *uke*. *Tori* then wraps their right arm around *uke*'s lead leg, clockwise, so that *tori*'s wrist rests at the back of *uke*'s heel (preferably just on the tendon). *Tori* then pushes his shoulder into *uke*'s leg, gently in practise as this puts a great deal of strain on the knee joint (in actual combat however...). This will cause *uke* to fall backwards and *tori* can continue his forward motion (very similar to a right-handed forward roll) rolling up to strike *uke*'s groin with his left fist or elbow (the choice of which should be obvious at that point).

49

Basic breaking of ground strangles (start position).

Basic breaking of ground strangles (i).

6. Basic Breaking of Ground Strangles

All three of these moves start with *uke* kneeling over *tori*, one knee either side of *tori*'s chest, and with both hands on *tori*'s throat. The first thing to be done in all cases is for *tori* to strike *uke*. The usual strike is to the kidneys or floating ribs with both hands simultaneously. This should have the effect of loosening the strangle (always a good thing!) and distracting your opponent from what you are about to do next.

(i) In this first escape *tori* moves his left arm over *uke*'s right and under *uke*'s left. This should leave *tori* with the back of his left hand behind *uke*'s left elbow. *Tori* then brings his right hand to join the left, palm to palm, and pushes to the left. While pushing with the hands on *uke*'s elbow *tori* needs to bring his hips off the floor, thus pushing with his legs as well as his arms. Once *uke* is over to the left *tori* finishes with a knee strike to the groin. The position of *tori*'s left arm at the beginning of

the technique has two main effects: first it causes *uke*'s right arm to bend (therefore removing *uke*'s support in the direction you are going to push) and second to lock *uke*'s left arm straight (giving the leverage to complete the technique).

(ii) The second of the escapes uses similar principles to the first. *Tori* uses his left hand to push down into the hollow of *uke*'s right elbow joint and at the same time pushes to the left on *uke*'s left elbow with his right hand. As with the first escape this bends *uke*'s right arm and locks their left arm straight. *Tori* thrusts up using his hips and finishes the escape in the same way as escape (i).

(iii) In the third of these escapes *tori* takes both of his arms underneath *uke*'s and grasps *uke*'s lapels. *Tori* then thrusts upwards with his hips and at the same time pulls *uke* forward (such that *tori*'s hands are aiming for a point a few inches above his own head). After propelling *uke*'s face into the floor *tori* finishes (if there is anything left to finish) with a knee strike to the base of *uke*'s spine. With this technique it is

Basic breaking of ground strangles (ii).

Basic breaking of ground strangles (iii).

Wrist throw (block and take).

Wrist throw (second hand take).

important to remember to turn your head to one side as you move *uke* (this prevents the painful sensation of feeling your nose spread across your face!).

7. Wrist Throw

This throw is shown here as a defence against a punch to the stomach. *Tori* performs a downward outside forearm block (*see* Chapter 3) and moves his right leg in a clockwise semicircle (pivoting on the left foot). *Tori* takes hold of *uke*'s right hand with his left hand. *Tori* should grip *uke*'s hand with his thumb on the back of the

Wrist throw (throw).

51

Shoulder armlock (block and wrap).

tori twists *uke*'s hand so that the palm faces towards *uke* and the fingertips rotate in an anticlockwise motion (as seen from the back of the hand).

This is a complicated throw and as such the description given is only the 'bare bones' of it. As such it will still work but to obtain the full benefit of the technique requires a great deal of practise with a good ju-jitsu (or *aikido*) *sensei*.

8. Shoulder Armlock

This armlock is shown as a defence against a right-handed punch to the face. *Tori* uses an inside forearm parry then wraps his left (blocking) arm around *uke*'s right (attacking) arm in an anticlockwise motion. As this is happening *tori* steps in with his right foot (placing it just to the left of *uke*'s right foot) and strikes *uke*'s right shoulder with a right palm heel. Leaving his right hand on *uke*'s shoulder *tori* brings his left hand up to rest on his own right wrist. As with the straight-arm lock described in the previous chapter *tori* needs to bring *uke* down to his level; the strike to the shoulder is

Shoulder armlock (lock).

hand (pointing in the same direction as *uke*'s fingers) and his fingers in *uke*'s palm, so that *tori*'s left hand is grasping the meat of *uke*'s thumb. *Tori* then brings his right hand to join the left (again: thumb on the back, fingers into the palm) and pivots on his right foot letting his left leg move in an anticlockwise semicircle. While doing this

Shoulder armlock from throw (arm wrap after throw).

Shoulder armlock from throw (lock).

intended to do this. Applying the lock consists of *tori* pushing downwards with both hands, straightening his arms slightly and leaning back a little with his shoulder. These are the motions you should get your muscles to aim for: if the lock is on tightly enough you will find that tensing your muscles to complete the motion is all that is needed (so no noticeable motion). The step with *tori*'s right foot helps with the lock but also prevents *uke* from delivering a kick to *tori* in the groin.

9. Shoulder Armlock from Throw

This technique starts, as its name suggests, with a basic throw from a right-hand punch (such as a hip throw or body drop). *Tori* keeps hold of *uke*'s right arm and *uke* should come to rest horizontally in front of him. *Tori* then kneels down so that his knees rest with one just behind *uke*'s ear and one on *uke*'s ribs. While kneeling *tori* allows *uke*'s right arm to slide up under his left armpit so that he ends up with *uke*'s arm held between his left arm and his body. *Tori* then places his right hand on *uke*'s right shoulder and brings his left arm underneath *uke*'s arm bringing his (*tori*'s) left hand up to rest on top of his own right wrist. To apply the lock *tori* leans his shoulder back slightly while at the same time pushing upwards with his left forearm (using the left hand on the wrist as a lever). It should be apparent from the name and, I hope, from practising this and the shoulder armlock in section eight that the lock is the same, just applied in a different situation. This is an important lesson: do not get hung up on only being able to do something from one position or stance; adapt to the situation and make the best of what is presented.

7 Orange Belt

1. One-Arm Shoulder Throw

Again using a left inside forearm parry in response to a right punch *tori* grasps *uke*'s attacking arm. *Tori* then steps in with the right foot, placing it next to *uke*'s right foot, and pivots on it in order to bring his left foot in next to the right. *Tori* needs to bend the knees while moving in and should end up facing in the same direction as *uke* with his feet parallel and inside *uke*'s. As he moves in *tori* needs to place his right arm under *uke*'s right arm so that *uke*'s arm rests on the crook of *tori*'s elbow. *Tori* bends his right arm, so that his hand is pointing upwards, thus using the crook of his elbow to hold *uke*'s arm. At this point there should be no gap between *uke* and

tori. *Tori* then completes the throw by simultaneously leaning forward, straightening the legs and pulling *uke* around his right-hand side. *Tori* needs to move his arms so that his hands end up at his left hip at the completion of the throwing motion.

2. Leg Throw with Lock

Parrying a right-hand punch to the face *tori* takes hold of the lower portion of *uke*'s lead leg with his right hand. At the same time *tori* strikes the top of the same leg at the front using a palm heel, aiming for just below the hip joint, and drives backwards and down. This strike combined with the pinning of the lower leg will cause *uke* to

One-arm shoulder throw (start position).

One-arm shoulder throw (throw).

fall backwards. *Tori* maintains his hold on *uke*'s lead leg and wraps his right arm around the calf area and forms a figure-four lock using the left arm (the arm position being the same as that for shoulder armlock in Chapter 6). To complete the pin and lock *tori* uses his nearest leg to pin *uke*'s free leg, using the heel on the nerves of the inner thigh (the anterior femoral nerve). This technique can be used without the lock (as circumstances dictate), going straight from throw to strikes (kick to groin, kick to floating ribs and kick to head using alternating feet).

Leg throw with lock (initial take).

3. Sweeping Loin Throw

There are two variations of this throw shown here (though numerous more exist). These vary only in the way *tori* moves in to do the throw, the throw itself is identical. It should be apparent that it is possible to apply this principle to most throws described.

(i) The first of the two, a defensive move, is sweeping loin from a punch. *Tori* uses an inside forearm parry against a right punch to the face and grabs *uke*'s attacking arm. *Tori* then steps in placing his right foot between *uke*'s feet, and then brings his left leg up alongside and slides his right arm around *uke*'s waist. At this point *tori* needs to be facing forward but with his right hip in contact with *uke* (lower abdomen or groin). *Tori* needs to have bent his left leg as he moves it in and now shifts his weight forward so that all of the weight is on his left leg. As *tori* leans forward he needs to maintain contact with *uke*, which should bring *uke* up onto his toes. *Tori* then brings his right foot forwards off the floor (pointing the toes downwards and to the left) then sweeps backwards with the leg while pulling *uke* around with his arms (as per

Leg throw with lock (lock).

Leg throw with lock (alternative with strikes).

Sweeping loin throw ((i) initial position).

Sweeping loin throw ((i) throw).

the one-arm shoulder throw). *Tori*'s sweeping leg needs to bisect *uke*'s right leg around the knee joint (accuracy comes with practise and will be needed as you will see in later chapters).

This throw, when done correctly, will have quite a spectacular effect on *uke*. However it will take practise and is one of the techniques that is very difficult to do slowly, or in parts. All throws are easier to do when performed in one flowing motion; however there are certain throws which rely on that continuous motion, and as such are usually bugbears for the student until the day it finally clicks into place (and trust me that it does, sooner or later).

(ii) Attacking sweeping loin on the other hand is, as it says, an attack for those occasions where you need to take a more proactive approach to defence. All that differs from the defensive sweeping loin described is that *tori* moves in before any attack from *uke*. *Tori* does this by stepping in with his right foot and striking with his right side. Shown here he moves in with an

elbow strike to the solar plexus. The strike is up to you but bear in mind the effect of the strike (the way in which your opponent's body will move) and where you want to end up. *Tori* takes hold of *uke*'s right arm with his left, places his right arm around *uke*'s waist and brings his left foot in behind the right. *Tori* is now in a position to execute the technique as described in (i).

4. Outer Reaping Throw

This throw is shown here from a right punch with *uke*'s right leg forward (as it would be in a lunge punch), which is the best way to start practising this throw. The throw can be done in the same way if *uke*'s left leg remained forward (though it takes more practise) but I find the left-handed version of the throw (from a right-hand punch) works better in such cases. If *uke*'s legs are parallel either technique can be used.

Tori needs to move into *uke*'s attack so that his left foot ends up level with, and outside, *uke*'s right foot. To do this *tori* uses

Outer reaping throw (block).

Outer reaping throw (strike and balance).

a more aggressive inside forearm parry. *Tori* needs to be intercepting *uke*'s arm before it has had any time to pick up speed, the nearer to its start point the better. Once in this position *tori* continues the motion of his left arm, pushing *uke*'s right arm back and to the left, taking him off balance, at the same time striking the left-hand side of *uke*'s neck with a ridge hand strike (*see* Chapter 2). The direction of the strike should be through *uke*'s neck and, as with the blocking arm, aim back and to the left. *Tori* then shifts his weight forward onto his left leg bringing his right leg off the floor and past the outside of *uke*'s right leg. *Tori* points the toes of his right foot down and to the left, and sweeps backwards against the back of *uke*'s right leg. Once it has been practised sufficiently you should try and bring the strike and sweep to the point where they are simultaneous.

Outer reaping throw (sweep).

Inner reaping throw (strike and balance).

Inner reaping throw (throwing position).

5. Inner Reaping Throw

This technique is shown using a cross block, one of the few 'true' blocks used in this style of ju-jitsu. As shown the block, using the right forearm (the forearm twisting so that *tori*'s little finger turns towards himself (anticlockwise looking downwards)), stops *uke*'s right punch. As described in the chapter on parries and blocks *tori* should end this block with his right leg forward. *Tori* then strikes the right-hand side of *uke*'s neck with a knife hand using his right (blocking) hand. As *tori* strikes he brings his left foot up to his right then extends his right leg forward between *uke*'s legs and around the back of *uke*'s left leg (see note). *Tori*'s right leg should be as far round as possible and be in contact with the back of *uke*'s leg, but *tori*'s leg should still be bent and his right foot should be up on its toes. While moving the leg into position *tori* needs to continue the motion of his knife hand strike and push *uke* backwards and to the right (rear right-hand diagonal). Once *tori* has *uke* in this off balance position with his leg behind *tori*

pushes sharply with his right arm on *uke*'s neck while at the same time putting his right heel on the floor and straightening his right leg sharply. Note: this technique is described with *uke* having his left leg forward or legs level; if *uke* had his right leg forward it would be more effective to use a left-handed version (regardless of which hand punched).

6. Double Armlock Hold from a Throw

This hold-down can be done from most throws but is probably easiest from a hip throw or a neck wheel throw (*see* Chapter 10). Once *tori* has thrown *uke* he maintains his hold on *uke*'s right arm with his left and places his right hand on *uke*'s forearm, pinning it to the floor (this should leave *uke* lying on his back). *Tori* then slides down into a sitting position next to *uke*'s right side with his right leg under *uke*'s right arm (uke's upper arm needs to be over *tori*'s right thigh). *Tori*'s right leg should be bent at the knee so that the lower portion points away from *uke* at a right angle. Using his left hand (which should still be in control of *uke*'s right arm) *tori* bends *uke*'s arm to form an L-shape with the hand facing away from them. This will allow *tori* to place *uke*'s upper arm underneath his own lower right leg (the lock on this arm is applied by lowering the lower right leg and raising the hips off the floor). Once *uke*'s right arm is in position *tori* grips *uke*'s left wrist with his left hand and again places his arm in an L-shape, hand facing away. *Tori* then slides his right hand under *uke*'s upper arm and places it either on top of his own left wrist or on top of *uke*'s wrist (this lock is applied by *tori* pulling his own hands towards *uke*'s bicep and raising his right elbow). For best effect both locks are applied simultaneously. To finish (if needed!) *tori* moves his right hand onto the top of *uke*'s left wrist (if he hadn't already) freeing his left hand, which takes *uke*'s right arm out and places it across so that *uke*'s hands come together. *Tori* uses his left hand to keep *uke* in place by putting pressure on *uke*'s right elbow and draws out his own right hand which he uses to strike to the ribcage.

7. Rice Bail Throw

For this technique *tori* parries a right punch to the face with his left arm then steps in with his right foot and strikes the right-hand side of *uke*'s neck with his right elbow. This should cause *uke* to bend his head forward slightly and *tori* uses this motion to allow him to wrap his right arm around *uke*'s neck. *Tori* then places his left hand over the back of his right hand ensuring that the bone of the wrist (radial, or thumb, side) is firmly in place on *uke*'s windpipe. *Tori* applies upward pressure on *uke*'s windpipe then places both feet together next to the outside of *uke*'s right

Double armlock hold from throw (hold).

foot. *Tori* maintains his grip and sits down, with his backside as close to his own feet as he can get. This should propel *uke* over the top (at this stage *tori* should use his left arm as a shield for his face), leaving him prone with the choke still on. To finish *tori* cups *uke*'s chin with his right hand and rolls to the right. This should roll *uke* likewise onto his front and leave *tori* with an obvious finish (if it isn't obvious at that point, ask your *sensei*).

An alternative start is to block as above but to then simultaneously punch *uke* to the solar plexus with the right hand while striking the back of his head with the flat of the left hand. This will bend *uke* into a position that will allow you to place your right arm around *uke*'s neck and complete the technique as described above.

8. Wrist Locks

(i) This first lock is shown from a right-handed push to *tori*'s left shoulder (a similar principle can be applied to a punch, and so on). The first thing *tori* needs to do

Rice bail throw (step and strike).

Rice bail throw (wrap neck).

Rice bail throw (throw).

Rice bail throw (alternative start).

is to step back with his left foot (the same foot as shoulder being pushed): this has two effects. The first is to absorb the power of the push, moving freely with it rather than resisting it. The second is to throw *uke* off balance, as he would be expecting some resistance. *Tori* then brings his right hand over the top of *uke*'s right hand and takes hold. *Tori*'s palm should be on the back of *uke*'s hand, his fingers should grip around next to *uke*'s little finger and into the palm, and *tori*'s thumb should grip around into the palm between *uke*'s thumb and forefinger. *Tori* then turns *uke*'s hand

so that its back is facing *tori* and places his left hand (over the top) into the hollow of *uke*'s right elbow (if *tori* turns his left shoulder back towards *uke* it helps the next part of the lock). To apply the lock *tori* rotates his right hand clockwise (twisting *uke*'s hand) and his left hand anticlockwise (bringing *uke*'s elbow down). Students of *aikido* will recognize aspects of *nikkyo* (*aikido*'s second immobilization) in this lock; considering the origins of the two arts this should surprise no one.

(ii) In this lock *uke* has pushed *tori*'s right shoulder with his right hand. Again *tori*

Wrist lock ((i) a).

Wrist lock ((i) b).

steps back with the foot on the attacked side (right in this case). *Tori* then reaches over *uke*'s attacking arm with his left hand and takes hold of *uke*'s right hand. As before the thumb goes to the back of *uke*'s hand and *tori*'s fingers curl around into the palm of *uke*'s hand. *Tori* then grasps *uke*'s attacking hand with his right, the grip mirroring that taken with his left, then he turns *uke*'s hand so that the palm faces towards *uke*'s body. At this point *tori* has a choice of continuing the motion and performing a wrist throw (*see* Chapter 6) or doing a static lock. To complete the lock *tori* merely rotates his hands, pushing forward with his thumbs and pulling back with his fingers. This will cause *uke*'s palm to rotate from facing *uke* to facing down at the floor leaving *uke*'s face in a very inviting position for a finish with the knee.

Wrist lock (ii).

Wrist lock (iii).

(iii) For this lock *uke* pushes directly at the centre of *tori*'s chest. *Tori* redirects the force by placing his right hand (edge-on, little finger downward) at the bend in *uke*'s attacking wrist and pushing downwards. At the same time *tori* uses his left hand to grab *uke*'s elbow, pulling towards himself to pin *uke*'s hand to him. Once *uke*'s hand is pinned to *tori*'s body (preferably around the stomach area) *tori* places his right hand on the elbow and, using both hands, pulls the elbow towards him. The motion should feel as though *tori* were trying to throw *uke*'s elbow over his own right shoulder.

9. Bar Chokes

The main difference between a choke and a strangle is that a choke puts pressure on the windpipe in order to stop air getting to the lungs, whereas a strangle puts pressure on the arteries (thus directly stopping oxygenated blood from getting to the brain). The finished product is the same, only the route differs. Bar chokes use *tori*'s forearm as a bar directly across the windpipe.

To use the *gi* (ju-jitsu suit) *tori* first grabs the right-hand side of *uke*'s collar with his right hand. With the fingers underneath and the thumb on top *tori* needs to reach as deep as possible with this grip. *Tori* then takes hold of *uke*'s left lapel with his left hand and puts his right forearm across *uke*'s throat. To apply *tori* pulls down with his left hand and twists his right forearm to bring his thumb to the underneath.

Without the *gi*, *tori* grabs *uke*'s neck with his left hand and places his right hand on his own left wrist. The right forearm is again placed across *uke*'s throat and the lock is applied by twisting the forearm in an upward motion.

10. Drawing Ankle Throw

This is one of those techniques that is very difficult to do slowly or bit by bit. It needs to be done in one motion as *uke*'s momentum is essential to the throw's success. *Uke* attacks with a right lunge punch, and at the same time *tori* steps, from a short fighting stance, forward and to the right with his right foot (at roughly a

Bar choke (with *gi*).

Bar choke (without *gi*).

forty-five degree angle). As they step *tori* parries *uke*'s right arm using his left. *Tori* takes hold with his left hand drawing *uke* forwards and at the same time places his left foot on the front of *uke*'s right ankle. *Tori*'s right hand is placed under *uke*'s left armpit and *tori* twists anticlockwise pulling *uke* with his left hand whilst pushing under the armpit with his right. As mentioned this needs to be one motion so that as *tori* steps with his right he is parrying with his left. As *tori*'s right foot has finished moving he should already be drawing *uke* forward with his left hand, starting to push under the armpit with his right and placing his left foot in position. It becomes apparent, once you practise this technique, why everything needs to move as one.

Drawing ankle throw.

11. Stamp Throw

A stamp throw can be used as a throw unto itself but it is primarily intended as a combination throw (*see* Chapter 12). A combination throw is used where the initial technique did not work, and rather than breaking free and starting again, *tori* alters his position and utilizes another technique. Here *tori* has moved in for a hip throw but *uke* has resisted by leaning back. Rather than disengage, *tori* maintains his hold and raises his right foot high while leaning slightly into *uke*. *Tori* tightens his grip then stamps downwards while pulling *uke* over, as per a hip throw. This works by using the powerful leg muscles to jar *uke*'s position, breaking his contact with the floor, and thus allowing the hip throw to be finished. Be warned, because *uke* is pulling back slightly the sudden release of tension when the stamp is performed can cause *uke* to be thrown faster than expected. It is the same principle as stretching an elastic band and then having someone cut it; the release can be painful!

Stamp throw (initial resistance).

Stamp throw (stamp).

Body scissors and choke (double strike).

Body scissors and choke (floor position).

12. Body Scissors and Choke

As its name suggests this technique combines a scissors move (using the legs) and a chokehold. *Uke* attacks with a right punch and *tori* performs an outside parry using his right hand while stepping forward and to the left with his right foot. *Tori* then simultaneously strikes *uke* with his left and right hands. *Tori*'s right hand strikes *uke*'s neck using a ridge hand strike while his left hand punches *uke* to the kidney. This causes *uke* to turn so that his back is to *tori*. *Tori* then sits down as close as possible to *uke* keeping his right arm around *uke*'s neck and his left hand in *uke*'s back. Sitting down will leave *uke* lying backwards over

tori's knees and *tori* now slowly opens his knees and brings his legs around *uke*'s chest. As he is doing this *tori* needs to bring his left hand up to join his right. *Tori*'s right hand should be across *uke*'s throat, palm downwards. *Tori* takes hold of his right hand with his left, palm to palm. *Tori* now links his legs, and from this position can apply pressure to *uke*'s ribcage while applying the choke. To finish *tori* rolls to his right using the back of his right hand on *uke*'s left cheek to encourage him to roll. As they are rolling *tori* needs to secure *uke*'s left arm with his now-free left hand. This will leave *uke* lying face down with *tori* on top in control of *uke*'s neck and left arm; finish off at your discretion!

8 Green Belt

1. Dropping Full Shoulder

This throw is shown here as a defence against a choke. *Uke* attacks from behind by wrapping his right arm around *tori*'s neck. *Tori* first takes hold of *uke*'s right arm at the crook of the elbow using his right hand and pulls it away from the throat. *Tori* then turns his hips so that they are at a right angle to *uke*'s body and at the same time strikes *uke*'s solar plexus with his left elbow (turning the hips opens up this target area). *Tori* then kneels down on his right knee while keeping tight hold of *uke*'s arm. Pulling forward from this position brings *uke* over *tori*'s back. The finish shown is quite simple to perform as the right arm is already in the right position (under *uke*'s right arm); *tori* merely places the first two fingers of his right hand on the far side of *uke*'s windpipe and straightens *uke*'s right arm over his arm.

Note: when kneeling to perform this technique it is important to move the right foot and place the right knee where the foot was. If *tori* kneels without moving his foot he will be kneeling too far in front of *uke* and the technique will not be as effective (try it for yourself).

2. Escapes from Bear Hugs

One common thread running through all the bear hug techniques shown here (and indeed through all escapes and quite a proportion of ju-jitsu techniques in general) is that they all start with distraction strikes. These strikes (and other techniques) are intended to momentarily distract *uke* thus allowing *tori* to complete his escape. These strikes are unlikely to be enough in themselves but do not underestimate their effectiveness.

Dropping full shoulder (weakener).

Dropping full shoulder (throw).

Dropping full shoulder (lock).

Escape from bear hug ((i) a).

Escape from bear hug ((i) b).

I have shown a bare (bear, sorry about the pun) minimum here amounting to eight techniques; the only real limit is the student's imagination. I have placed them in a set order according to the style of attack: underarm from behind ((i) and (ii)); overarm from behind ((iii) and (iv)); underarm from the front ((v) and (vi)) and overarm from the front ((vii) and (viii)).

(i) In this first escape the distraction strike uses the second knuckle of the second finger to strike a nerve point on the back of *uke*'s hand (*see* Chapter 2). *Tori* then takes hold of *uke*'s left hand (in this case the upper hand) with his thumbs on the back of the hand. *Tori* turns and steps, with his right foot, out to *uke*'s left then brings his left foot round anticlockwise to join his right. While moving *tori* needs to move *uke*'s hand so that the fingers now face upwards and the palm faces towards *uke*. *Tori* applies the lock by rotating his hands, thumbs forward and fingers back, and finishes with a kick to *uke*'s face.

(ii) In this escape *tori* slides the side of his right foot down *uke*'s shin bringing the heel down sharply onto *uke*'s right foot. *Tori* bends his knees (keeping his heel on

uke's foot) which pins *uke*'s right leg. *Tori* then reaches between his own legs, grabs *uke*'s right leg with both hands and (after taking his heel off *uke*'s foot) pulls the leg forwards and upwards thus depositing *uke* on the floor. The finish is a simple left kick to an obvious target.

(iii) For this escape *tori* takes hold of the arms that are themselves holding him; this is done before any strikes. *Tori* then strikes *uke* to the groin with a back heel kick. Keeping a tight grip on *uke*'s arms *tori* then turns ninety degrees to his left and stamps his raised right foot down while drawing *uke* over his back. It sounds simple but this one does require quite a bit of practise.

(iv) The distraction for this technique comes from a backwards head strike. *Tori* then leaves his right foot in place but moves his left foot to the right then round behind *uke*. Once in this position *tori* turns anticlockwise and leans back taking *uke* over his left hip. The choice between escape (iii) and (iv) is one of balance. If *uke* has taken hold and his weight is bearing forward then (iii) is the obvious choice; if he is leaning back then (iv). If there is no bias the choice is yours.

Escape from bear hug ((ii) a).

Escape from bear hug ((ii) b).

Escape from bear hug ((iii) a).

Escape from bear hug ((iii) b).

Escape from bear hug ((iv) a).

Escape from bear hug ((iv) b).

Escape from bear hug ((v) a).

Escape from bear hug ((v) b).

Escape from bear hug (vi).

(v) Being held under the arms and from the front gives *tori* open season on strikes and I have picked one of my favourites to show. The target is *uke*'s kidneys and the strike is a double knife hand. To increase effectiveness *tori* needs to cup both of his hands upwards when striking. The first escape then involves *tori* bringing the side of his right hand up underneath *uke*'s nose and pushing backwards. There are plenty of embellishments that can be added: stepping between *uke*'s legs, grabbing *uke*'s groin with the other hand and so on.

(vi) From the same initial strike as in (v) *tori* turns anticlockwise taking hold of *uke*'s neck with his right arm and grasping *uke*'s right arm with his left hand. Completing the turn and bending the knees puts *tori* in a position to do a variation of a hip throw.

Escape from bear hug ((vii) a).

Escape from bear hug ((vii) b).

Escape from bear hug (viii).

Knee wheel.

(vii) Owing to the restricting nature of this hold the kidney strike may not have the desired effect, hence a second strike may be necessary. Once an effective strike has been put in place *tori* turns to perform a hip throw but with two slight differences. The first is that *tori* needs to grab *uke*'s right arm from underneath with his left. The second is that *tori*'s right arm does not grab *uke*'s waist (as in a normal hip throw) but grips *uke*'s left arm, at the shoulder joint, in a similar way to the grip used in a one-arm shoulder throw (we will see this grip again in the hip wheel in Chapter 9).

(viii) For this escape *tori* strikes as per the description in (vii) then places his right foot between *uke*'s feet. *Tori* leans down and grabs the back of *uke*'s knees (taking a good hold on the tendons). To execute the throw *tori* pulls *uke*'s knees apart and slightly towards them. A finishing strike should present itself.

3. Knee Wheel

For this technique first read the description of a drawing ankle throw in the previous chapter. The throw is identical in

Variation of shoulder throw ((i) a).

Variation of shoulder throw ((i) b).

Variation of shoulder throw ((ii) a).

Variation of shoulder throw ((ii) b).

everything except the position of *tori*'s left foot. In this throw *tori*'s left foot is placed at the knee and the throw is executed as per the drawing ankle throw. Which of these two very similar throws is used will depend on *uke* and *tori*'s relative positions once the attack and parry has been done.

4. Variations of Shoulder Throw

These variations are, as their name suggests, only slightly different from a basic one-arm shoulder throw. They incorporate

other throws with the one-armed shoulder throw to allow for circumstances where the normal version either would not work or would be inadvisable.

(i) This first variation is the lapel shoulder throw. After using a left inside forearm parry *tori* takes hold of *uke*'s left-hand lapel with his right hand. This is done in the form of a strike then grab, striking with the palm heel to the left of *uke*'s chest then grabbing the lapel. The feet and body movements are now performed in the same way as for the normal one-arm shoulder throw, the difference being how the right arm is used. As *tori* is moving in for the throw he points his right elbow out to his left, placing his right arm under *uke*'s right arm. In the lapel half-shoulder *tori* brings *uke* straight over, rather than up and around as in the regular throw. If the throw feels awkward it may be because *uke*'s *gi* is tight; in that case try taking a lower grip on the lapel.

(ii) The variation shown here is a dropping version of the lapel shoulder thow (i). *Tori* performs a lapel half-shoulder but with slightly different footwork. The footwork is the same as that for a body drop (*see* Chapter 6): *tori* needs to end up with the back of his right knee touching the front of *uke*'s leg (as shown). *Tori* should slightly bend this knee, without any loss of contact with *uke*'s leg, and then straighten it sharply as he pulls *uke* forwards and around.

(iii) This variation combines the one-arm shoulder throw with the stamp throw leg movements. *Tori* goes in for the shoulder throw, meets resistance, then uses his right leg to overcome it as described for a stamp throw (*see* Chapter 7) whilst maintaining the half-shoulder grip.

(iv) and (v) These variations are the body drop shoulder throw and dropping body drop shoulder throw respectively. The body drop shoulder throw requires the arm movements of a regular one-arm shoulder throw and the footwork of a body drop (*see* Chapter 6). The dropping body drop shoulder throw requires a slightly different movement, involving dropping down onto the left knee (*see* the dropping body drop in Chapter 9). The picture shows the leg positions, kneeling on the left knee with the right leg extended. The use of the arms and right leg are the same as for previous techniques, the difference comes from the lower body position. As a

Variation of shoulder throw (iii).

Variation of shoulder throw (iv).

Variation of shoulder throw (v).

Variation of shoulder throw ((vi) a).

Variation of shoulder throw ((vi) b).

Variation of shoulder throw (vii).

general rule with this class of throw (hip throws, shoulder throws, and body drop throws) *tori* needs to get his hips below *uke*'s centre of balance (in most cases the knot of the *obi* (belt) is a very close estimate (handy!)) and the lower *tori* gets, the faster the throw will be.

(vi) In this throw the variation from a standard one-arm shoulder throw is in the initial defence. *Tori* blocks the inside of *uke*'s right forearm with a right-hand cross block (a definite block rather than a parry). *Tori* takes hold of *uke*'s right arm with his left and uses a right-hand backfist to strike *uke*'s floating ribs. From here the one-arm shoulder throw is performed as normal.

(vii) This is a sweeping shoulder throw. As its name suggests it combines the sweeping loin with the shoulder throw. This means that *tori* steps in half-hip, using the one-arm shoulder throw arm work to bring *uke* to his toes, and then sweeps.

It should be apparent from the descriptions of these variations that the only limit to the number of variations is the imagination of the student. Remember that there is a reason for these variations; that there are circumstances under which the basic throws are not appropriate. This fact has a wider implication for the student; these throws are slightly different to the originating throws and as such require practise in their own right. Do not believe that because you can do a one-arm shoulder throw and a body drop that you can automatically perform a body drop shoulder throw. Practise with the basic throws makes the variations easier to master than completely fresh techniques, but do not get complacent. A good student should be aiming to be able to flow between different techniques and adapt combinations of throws at will. The goal is to do this without thinking, to let your body 'remember' what it needs. This has been stated by two great martial artists (at least), each in their own way. The first was Musashi, in referring to 'attitude, no attitude', and the second was Bruce Lee who said 'what you have learnt is meant to be forgotten...'. The more you practise the more this will make sense to you.

5. Variations of Chokes

Shown here are variations of chokes and strangles. As mentioned a choke is designed to cut off the air supply to the lungs by attacking the throat and a strangle is designed to cut off the blood supply to the brain. Have a look and see if you can decide for yourself which category each technique falls into.

(i) The first choke shown is the naked chokehold. This calls for *tori* to place his right forearm across *uke*'s throat with the palm of the hand facing downwards. Next *tori* grabs his right hand with his left hand, palm to palm, left palm facing upwards. The choke is applied by *tori* drawing his right forearm backwards while at the same time twisting it so that the edge in contact with *uke*'s throat moves upwards.

(ii) The second choke shown here is a variation of the naked choke. With the arms in the same position as for the choke in (i) *tori* then places the top of his head at the base of *uke*'s skull before applying the lock.

(iii) For this lock *tori* again places his right forearm across the front of *uke*'s throat but this time he places his right palm on his left bicep and puts his left palm on the back of *uke*'s head. The lock is applied by bringing both elbows back and pushing *uke*'s head forwards. As a variation place

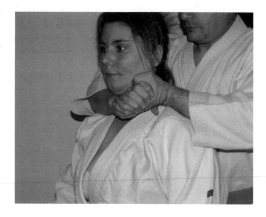

Variation of choke (i).

Variation of choke (ii).

Variation of choke (iii).

Variation of choke (iv).

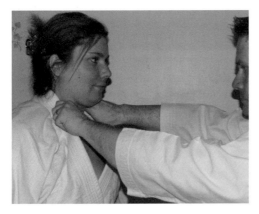

Variation of choke (v).

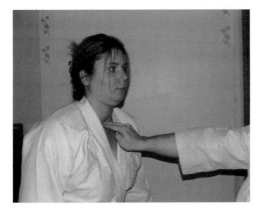

Variation of choke (vi).

your right arm around *uke*'s neck such that your elbow is in-line with the point of his chin.

(iv) In this lock *tori* places his right hand around *uke*'s neck and grabs as high up on *uke*'s left side collar as possible. *Tori* then brings his left hand up under *uke*'s left arm and places his palm on the back of *uke*'s head. The lock is again applied by bringing the elbows back and pushing *uke*'s head forward.

(v) Taking hold of both sides of *uke*'s collar, thumbs inside, *tori* turns both hands so that the thumbs become visible while pushing the knuckles into *uke*'s neck. Be careful as this can be quite a powerful lock.

(vi) This technique only requires the first and second finger of one hand. The fingers are placed over the top of the sternum, pushed into the throat, and then hooked downwards.

(vii) This technique is called, colourfully, the butterfly choke by some. *Tori* crosses his thumbs over to form a 'V' (the idea behind the name is that his open hands now take on the appearance of a butterfly: use your imagination!). The thumbs are then placed over *uke*'s windpipe so that the junction of the thumbs touches the front of the windpipe. *Tori* then scissors the thumbs together around *uke*'s windpipe.

(viii) This technique uses just the thumb and forefinger of one hand. *Tori* presses his thumb and forefinger down on either side of the windpipe and then closes them together around the windpipe itself. Be very careful with this one, boys and girls; there is cartilage behind the windpipe that can be damaged very easily.

(ix) In this technique *tori* uses only one hand. The fingers and thumb of the hand need to be closed and flat. *Tori* now places the outside of his forefinger at a forty-five degree angle on the opposite side of the throat from him, with the fingers pointing to the ground (shown in the picture *tori* is using his right hand, kneeling on *uke*'s right side and is placing the forefinger on the left side of *uke*'s throat). *Tori* then slides the hand, at the forty-five degree angle, towards the floor. The choke comes on when *tori*'s thumb comes into contact with the near side of *uke*'s windpipe and pushes it sideways and down.

This is just a small selection of chokes and strangles and as with many of the subjects here I could spend an entire book dedicated to this alone. I am sure your own *sensei* will have a few of their own that they will be more than happy to show you (just be warned: you will most likely be the victim of the demonstration!)

6. Escapes from a Full Nelson

For these escapes (and the half nelson escapes shown afterwards) I have used the wrestling term for the hold from which you seek to escape. I make no apologies for this as I believe it assists in understanding, the term being so well known.

The first of the escapes involves taking *uke* backwards and the second involves throwing him forwards; we have already discussed the reasons for the choice of direction.

(i) *Tori* first needs to use a weakener and in this position a back heel to the groin or a kick to the shins would work wonders. Next *tori* brings his hands down, breaking *uke*'s hold. *Tori* then moves his left foot behind *uke*, while leaving his right foot in place, and brings his left arm back across *uke*'s chest, turning his upper body anti-clockwise at the same time.

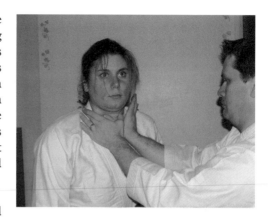

Variation of choke (vii).

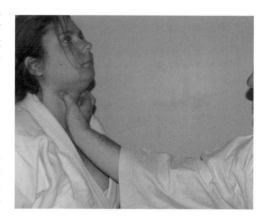

Variation of choke (viii).

Variation of choke (ix).

Escape from full nelson ((i) a).

Escape from full nelson ((i) b).

Escape from full nelson ((i) c).

Escape from full nelson ((ii) a).

Escape from full nelson ((ii) b).

(ii) In the second of these techniques *tori* weakens *uke* and breaks the grip as before but this time he retains the grip on *uke*'s arms (hooking the forearms under *uke*'s elbows is a good way of doing this). Keeping a tight grip on *uke*, *tori* turns a quarter of a turn anticlockwise, pushing his backside out to *uke*'s right. *Tori* then raises his right leg and stamps it down a foot or so further out from its start position while drawing *uke* forwards, using his arms, over his back (you should be spotting a similarity here to an escape from a bear hug earlier).

Escape from half nelson ((i) a).

Escape from half nelson ((i) b).

7. Escapes from a Half Nelson

(i) *Tori* begins this escape with a side snap kick to the side of *uke*'s knee. *Tori* then takes hold of *uke*'s left wrist with his left hand and places his right hand just under *uke*'s left elbow. From this position *tori* pushes *uke*'s elbow upwards and rotates it forwards before bringing it down in front of him. As the elbow is being moved *tori* needs to bring his left hand down to his left hip (while still maintaining his grip on *uke*'s left wrist). From here *tori* can apply a lock by applying direct pressure down onto *uke*'s elbow (using a straight arm and having *uke*'s elbow at *tori*'s centre) or by pushing his right forearm down onto *uke*'s shoulder joint and raising his left hand. Both techniques are effective, though in different ways: try both and discover which you prefer.

Escape from half nelson ((i) c).

Escape from half nelson ((iii) a).

Escape from half nelson ((iii) b).

Back scissors (initial leg position).

Back scissors (throw).

(ii) In the second escape *tori* uses the same side snap kick weakener but this time uses this to allow him to perform a back scissors throw. As before the outside leg is rotated anticlockwise and placed behind *uke*'s legs and the inside leg scissors backwards, striking *uke* around the waist or above. For a fuller description of the back scissors throw along with the pictures see the next section.

(iii) In this third escape *tori* uses a left-handed strike to the groin, which bends *uke* forwards, or the thigh. *Tori* then steps between *uke*'s legs from behind with his right leg and places it across the front of *uke*'s right shin. *Tori*'s right leg needs to be slightly bent but still in firm contact with *uke*'s leg. *Tori* then takes hold of *uke*'s lower left leg. To complete the throw *tori* simultaneously pulls *uke*'s left leg backwards and straightens his own right leg.

8. Back Scissors Throw

This technique is shown as a defence against a right punch to the stomach. *Tori* parries the outside of *uke*'s forearm using his left arm and takes hold of it. *Tori* then

Front scissors (initial leg position).

Front scissors (throw).

places his right hand on the floor to steady himself while at the same time sweeping his right leg around, clockwise, coming to rest behind *uke*'s legs. *Tori* brings his left leg up and backwards, striking *uke* around the stomach area. The throw is performed by 'scissoring' the legs, left leg backwards and right leg forwards. Obviously the bigger the gap between the left and right foot, the more leverage is applied to *uke*'s body. To finish *tori* maintains the grip on *uke*'s left wrist and strikes to *uke*'s sternum with a right bottom fist.

Note: placing the right hand on the floor during this technique is only meant to assist while learning the throw, with practice it becomes unnecessary.

9. Front Scissors Throw

Uke attacks here with a right punch which *tori* parries with an outside forearm parry. As he is parrying *tori* needs to step forward with his right leg until it is level with the outside of *uke*'s right foot. *Tori* then places his left hand on the floor for balance and brings his left leg in an anticlockwise circle

until it comes to rest in front of *uke*'s legs. *Tori* then brings his right leg up and back, striking *uke* in the small of the back and propelling him forwards. When *uke* lands *tori* needs to place his right ankle at the back of *uke*'s right knee and then place *uke*'s right leg upright running up his chest. *Tori* then leans forward (the feeling is as if you were to place *uke*'s right heel at the base of his spine).

10. Downward Inside Forearm Block

This simple block is shown here as a left-handed block to a right-handed punch to the stomach. From the short fighting stance *tori* brings his left arm down in a clockwise arc, twisting the arm as it comes down so that the back of his blocking hand ends up facing to the right. This means that *tori* is blocking using the muscle of his inside forearm rather than the bone. As *tori* brings the blocking arm down he needs to bring his left shoulder forward and draw his right shoulder back. *Tori* then reverses his torso movement (drawing

Defence against front kicks (block and take).

Counter to bar choke ((i) a).

Counter to bar choke ((i) b).

back the left shoulder and twisting the right one forwards) and uses this motion to power a right punch to *uke*'s solar plexus. The block on its own is described in Chapter 3.

11. Defence against Front Kicks

This is covered further in Chapter 12 but I have included an extra defence here. This is the first point at which you would be expected to demonstrate a good proficiency with these defences.

Here *tori* uses the block described in section ten to block *uke*'s right front snap kick attack. *Tori* then takes hold of *uke*'s leg with his left hand and steps forward with his left foot. *Tori* then strikes *uke*'s sternum with a right palm heel strike while at the same time moving forward to bring his right leg between *uke*'s legs. *Tori* then sweeps backwards against the back of *uke*'s left leg with his right. Once *uke* is brought down *tori* can then finish off with a strike to his groin.

12. Counters to Bar Chokes

The first two escapes shown are from bar chokes using the *gi* and the second two from bar chokes without the *gi*.

(i) Here *tori* uses a right punch to *uke*'s floating ribs as a weakener while at the same time taking hold of *uke*'s left wrist with his own left hand (Taking hold of *uke*'s wrist has two uses here: the first is that *tori* has hold of it for the rest of the technique and the second is to take the choke off). *Tori* then places his right palm under *uke*'s left elbow (fingers pointing back). *Tori* then rotates *uke*'s elbow up, forwards and then down. Keeping his right hand on *uke*'s elbow *tori* applies the lock by

Counter to bar choke ((ii) a).

Counter to bar choke ((ii) b).

Counter to bar choke ((iii) a).

Counter to bar choke ((iii) b).

dropping his right elbow and raising his left hand, bringing *uke*'s left arm almost vertical.

(ii) The second escape starts with the same weakener to *uke*'s floating ribs. *Tori* then brings his left leg behind *uke*'s legs in order to perform a back scissors throw (I'm not describing it again!).

(iii) For this and (iv) the escape is shown for *uke* applying a bar choke with his left arm forming the bar, you will need to reverse the techniques for a right bar choke. *Tori* uses a punch to the solar plexus as a weakener while taking hold of

uke's left hand with his own left. Pinning *uke*'s left hand *tori* places his right palm on *uke*'s elbow, fingers pointing backwards, and moves it up and forwards. As this is happening *tori* extends his right leg out in front of *uke*'s right leg, knee bent with the back of the knee in contact with *uke*'s leg. Continuing the push on *uke*'s left elbow *tori* straightens his right leg sharply. Once *uke* hits the floor *tori* can use a strike to finish off if necessary.

(iv) For this escape *tori* takes hold of *uke*'s right wrist with his left hand and then uses a right palm heel strike to *uke*'s chin,

Entangled armlock (initial arm position).

Entangled armlock (lock).

striking upwards between *uke*'s arms. *Tori* then brings his right hand back, over the top of *uke*'s right arm, to take hold of *uke*'s right hand (thumb on the back, fingers into the palm). *Tori* performs the *nikkyo*-style wrist lock described in Chapter 7.

13. Entangled Armlock

Tori blocks a right punch to the stomach using a left downward inside forearm block and then reaches across with his right hand to take hold of *uke*'s right elbow. *Tori* then pushes back with his left arm while pulling *uke*'s elbow forward, thus bending the arm. *Tori* then pivots on his left foot and brings his right foot around, clockwise, so that he ends up facing the same way as *uke*. While turning *tori* continues the pull on *uke*'s elbow while bringing his left arm up under *uke*'s forearm so that *uke*'s forearm rests in the crook of *tori*'s elbow and *tori*'s hand rests on *uke*'s shoulder joint. *Tori* then pulls *uke*'s right elbow in so that it rests just behind his left hip. The lock is complete at this point but if it needs to be applied further *tori* can easily accomplish this by placing the fingers of his right hand into the hollow between the front of *uke*'s shoulder muscle and his pectoral muscle and applying pressure there (keep *uke* in the horizontal position while applying pressure to this nerve area to enhance the lock).

14. Combination of a Straight-Arm Lock

This is just one of many, but worth including at this point. In the purple belt we will look at ways for *tori* to counter *uke* by applying a straight-arm lock (*see* Chapter 5) but here we will look at one simple way for *tori* to move from a straight-arm lock which is being countered into a different

Combination of a straight-arm lock
(initial turn after resistance).

Combination of a straight-arm lock
(lock).

technique (a combination technique in other words).

In this technique *tori* moves in to a position to perform the straight-arm lock, on the outside of *uke*'s right arm, but *uke* resists by bending this arm. This is the most common form of resistance you will come across and works on instinct; if *uke* feels *tori* trying to bend the arm in one way his natural instinct is to bend the arm the opposite way.

In all techniques we use this natural instinct against the attacker but in this technique we have one of the most obvious. As *uke* bends their arm *tori* suddenly changes the direction of the force that he is applying. To apply the straight-arm lock *tori* has hold of *uke*'s right wrist and pushes it downwards (up against the bar of *tori*'s left arm which is positioned under *uke*'s arm). When *uke* resists this *tori* goes with *uke*'s movement and pushes up with *uke*'s wrist and turns towards him (thus for a fraction of a second *uke* is helping us by moving his arm with us) causing *uke*'s arm to move into an upright L-shape. As *tori* is doing this he moves his left hand across to take hold of the top of his own right wrist. *Tori* now has *uke* in a figure-four armlock as described in Chapter 6.

9 Blue Belt

1. Hip Wheel

For this throw *uke* attacks with a right punch to the face and *tori* uses a right-hand inside forearm parry and takes hold of *uke*'s right arm with his left hand. Once he has parried *tori* places his left foot just in front of and between *uke*'s legs. *Tori* then moves in placing his right arm under *uke*'s left armpit with his hand pointing upwards, gripping *uke*'s arm at the shoulder joint using the crook of his elbow. When moving in it is important that *tori* leaves his left foot where it has been placed and pivots around it. *Tori* brings his right leg in and around his left leg (anticlockwise). The foot will end up near to the point it started from (having gone around his left leg). It is important that this turn be completed in one smooth motion and that *tori* tightens up his grip on *uke* as he turns. Doing this means that when the right foot is brought down *uke* is pulled forward and over *tori*'s back (the 'wheel' part of the technique). This is another of those throws that is difficult to do slowly or in sections.

2. Escapes from a Headlock

(i) The headlock, as you can see, involves *uke* placing one arm around *tori*'s neck keeping him bent over. A headlock like this is usually accompanied by liberal use, by *uke*, of their other hand to punish *tori*'s face. Because of this it is imperative to immobilize *uke*'s free arm first. This is done by gripping it, from behind *uke*'s back, at the crook of the elbow. Shown here *uke* has hold of *tori*'s neck in his right arm so *tori* uses his left hand to immobilize *uke*'s free left arm. *Tori* then uses his right hand to attract *uke*'s attention. Here this is

Hip wheel (initial take).

Hip wheel (turn).

Hip wheel (throw).

Escape from headlock ((i) a).

Escape from headlock ((i) b).

Escape from headlock ((i) c).

Escape from headlock (ii).

by pinching the middle of the back of *uke*'s right thigh (in reality grabbing a good handful of the thigh around the sciatic nerve). Once this takes *uke*'s attention away from punching *tori* and moves him as shown *tori* brings his left hand over (around to the right-hand side of *uke*'s neck) and pushes the edge of it up under *uke*'s nose. This action bends *uke* backwards and opens up the solar plexus for a knife hand strike.

(ii) In this second escape *tori* uses a punch to the top of the outside of *uke*'s thigh to distract, attacking the common perenial or lateral femoral nerve (one being roughly one-third of the way down the thigh, the other two-thirds). *Tori* then pushes his left leg between *uke*'s legs, bending the knee and placing it firm against the front of *uke*'s left leg. *Tori* then pulls *uke*'s right leg back using his right hand and at the same time *tori* sharply straightens his left leg. The left hand can be used at this point in the small of *uke*'s back to help propel him forward. Finish off at will.

(iii) Here *tori* starts with the same weakener as for (ii) but then grabs as high up on *uke*'s right arm as possible with his right

Escape from headlock ((iii) a).

Escape from headlock ((iii) b).

Escape from headlock ((iv) a).

Escape from headlock ((iv) b).

hand, placing his left hand over the thigh to stop it moving and to parry other attacks if necessary. *Tori* leaves his right leg where it is and brings his left leg around to the front, putting his left foot in front of and in between *uke*'s feet. *Tori* keeps a tight grip and kneels down on his right knee, pulling *uke* around with his right hand. If necessary *tori* can assist the throw by striking backwards at *uke*'s left shin with his left hand.

(iv) After the weakener to the thigh *tori* bends his knees, allowing his to straighten his back, and moves his left hand around to the front of *uke*. *Tori* then strikes backwards with the left elbow, turning his torso in an anticlockwise direction and throwing himself (and consequently *uke*) backwards. *Tori* finishes with a complimentary left elbow strike to the solar plexus of the now recumbent (and stunned) *uke*.

(v) This escape is shown from a frontal headlock from the front with *uke* using his right arm to wrap around *tori*'s neck. *Tori* uses his right hand to strike at *uke*'s groin while taking the pressure off the choke with his left hand. *Tori* now takes hold of *uke*'s right hand with his, thumb on the

Escape from headlock ((v) a).

Escape from headlock ((v) b).

back and fingers in the palm, and places his left hand in the crook of *uke*'s right elbow. From here *tori* steps forward with his right leg, stepping to the outside of *uke*'s right leg, while maintaining their hold on *uke*'s right wrist and elbow. *Tori* straightens and turns anticlockwise so that he is now facing the same direction as *uke*. As he does this *tori* needs to keep the wrist at the same level while bringing *uke*'s elbow down to this same level. This straightens the arm and further pressure will apply the lock.

(vi) Starting with *uke* holding *tori* in a frontal headlock as for (v), *tori* strikes *uke* to the groin. *Tori* then takes hold of *uke*'s legs, just behind the knees, and steps forward with his right leg. Pulling *uke*'s legs apart (as opposed to lifting them) causes *uke* to fall backwards, giving *tori* an opening for a finishing strike. Stepping forward before the throw means that *tori* presents a slimmer cross-section to *uke*. This combined with the outward motion on *uke*'s legs stops *uke* from kicking *tori* to the groin on his way down (something to which those who have made this mistake in

practise can testify!). This finish is the same as for an escape from bear hugs (viii) in Chapter 8.

3. Defence against Garrotting

(i) This first garrotting is shown here from the front. The first two things *tori* must do need to happen simultaneously. *Tori* must use one hand to take pressure off his neck, by placing his fingers between the garrotte and his own neck (or restraining one of *uke*'s arms), while using the other hand to place a strike at *uke*. This takes the pressure off *tori*'s neck and allows time to perform a technique. Here *tori* has used his right hand to strike *uke*'s solar plexus; he then brings the right arm up and to the right, against the inside of *uke*'s left arm. At the same time *tori* brings his left arm down and to the left against the inside of *uke*'s right arm; this separates the arms (further taking the pressure off his neck). *Tori* takes hold of *uke*'s right arm with his left and takes hold of *uke*'s left lapel with his right hand and then turns into a hip

Defence against garrotting ((i) a).

Defence against garrotting ((i) b).

Defence against garrotting ((i) c).

Defence against garrotting ((ii) a).

Defence against garrotting ((ii) b).

throw, raising his right elbow under *uke*'s left armpit to give leverage to the throw.

Note: in this technique I have described one way of separating *uke*'s arms (to release the strangle). The way I have described works when the garrotte is held such that *uke* has to cross his hands to apply the strangle. Where *uke* has crossed the garrotte and applies it without crossing his arms using the above method would result in tightening the garrotte. To complete this throw in such a case *tori* must 'unwind' the garrotte by pushing up on the

Straight-arm bar takedown (strike and take).

Straight-arm bar takedown (throw).

elbow of the hand holding the top part of the garrotte and pushing down on the elbow of the hand underneath.

(ii) This second escape uses the inner reaping throw. *Tori* begins by striking *uke*'s chin up and backwards by using a palm heel strike with his right hand, the strike coming up between *uke*'s arms. At the same time *tori* moves his right foot between *uke*'s legs and hooks his right leg around *uke*'s left leg. The throw is then executed by *tori* straightening his right leg and pushing backwards with his right hand on *uke*'s chin.

(iii) This escape is from a rear garrotting; again, the two priorities being to take pressure off the neck and to strike *uke*. In this case *tori* pivots to the right and uses a right elbow to *uke*'s solar plexus. Continuing the turn until they are facing *uke*, *tori* then extends his right leg slightly and takes hold of the outside of *uke*'s knees. (This throw is the same as that described in section two (vi) of this chapter, escapes from a frontal headlock.)

(iv) This second escape from a rear garrotte begins as per (iii), with the right

elbow strike, but this time *tori* leaves himself facing the same way as *uke*. After the strike *tori* slides his right arm around *uke*'s waist and extends his right leg. This throw should be familiar as it is a body drop as described in Chapter 6.

Note: for all of the throws from an attack with a garrotte it is important to let your head follow *uke* nearly to the floor. The reason for this is that *uke* has a cord, rope or something similar around your neck and will probably still have hold of it. The result of not lowering your head is pain for yourself (as you suddenly receive all of *uke*'s weight on your neck) and reduced effectiveness of the throw as *uke* uses your neck to slow his descent!

4. Straight-Arm Bar Takedown

Uke attacks with a right punch to the face and *tori* steps forward and to the left with his right foot using a right-hand outside parry to deflect the attack. Taking hold of *uke*'s right wrist with his right hand *tori* then pulls *uke*'s right arm straight, steps in

89

Dropping body drop (initial take).

Dropping body drop (kneel).

Dropping body drop (throw).

with his left foot and strikes the side of *uke*'s chin with his left palm heel. *Tori* should now be standing side-on to *uke* with *uke*'s right arm straight out to the side and *tori*'s left upper arm tight up against *uke*'s neck. To complete the throw *tori* stretches his arms as far apart as he can while extending his left leg out in front and lowering his weight down on *uke*'s extended arm in order to pull *uke* over his left hip. Note, *tori*'s weight must be directed forward at this point otherwise sliding his left leg out to the front will result in him falling on his backside while *uke* remains standing (embarrassing in training but slightly more important a lapse in real combat!). Once on the floor *tori* is in a comfortable position to apply wrist and arm locks.

5. Dropping Version of a Body Drop

Uke attacks with a right punch to the face and *tori* uses a right-hand cross block. *Tori* then takes hold of *uke*'s right hand with his left and performs a downward backfist to *uke*'s groin with his right hand. *Tori* places his right hand in *uke*'s right armpit (thumb to the front, fingers to the rear) and pivots on his right foot, placing his left foot just outside and near enough level with *uke*'s left foot. By keeping his right arm straight this will push *uke* off balance to his right. *Tori* lowers his left leg until kneeling and extends his right leg across in front of *uke*'s legs. It is important to keep the toes of the right foot facing forward to prevent possible injury to the right knee if *uke* falls. *Tori* completes the throw by extending his right arm further to the right and pulling *uke*'s right arm across the front of his body to the left. It is possible to do this with the right leg straight or slightly bent (*see* the body drop in Chapter 6).

6. Spring Hip Throw

Here is another of those deceptively easy throws that needs to be done in a continuous motion. *Tori* uses a left inside forearm parry against *uke*'s right punch to the face. *Tori* then takes hold of *uke*'s right arm with his left hand, places his right foot directly between *uke*'s feet and puts his right arm around *uke*'s waist. *Tori* then lowers himself slightly, brings his body up into contact with *uke*'s middle, brings his left foot up to join the right (tori is at a right angle to *uke*) and starts to bring his body up again. The part that requires practise is the 'spring'. If the down, in and up motion is performed correctly it should bring *uke* up onto his tiptoes (it is possible to do the throw with only this motion, but that takes quite some practise, let's get the basics right first). As *tori* is coming up (and raising *uke*) he needs to transfer his balance to his left foot and bring his right foot off the floor. The right leg needs to be bent, the knee pointing out to the right, with the toes pointing downwards and the instep on the inside of *uke*'s right leg. The throw is completed using the arm motions of a hip throw while straightening the right leg (keeping it in contact with *uke*'s leg at all times).

Spring hip throw (initial step).

Spring hip throw (throwing position).

7. Scooping Throws

(i) The back scoop (or rear scoop) describes *uke*'s motion, and with this throw he goes backwards. *Uke* attacks with a right punch to the face but *tori* moves forward on his left foot, bringing it level with the outside of *uke*'s right foot, using a left inside forearm parry. To do this successfully *tori* must intercept the striking arm before it has time to move very far and keep the motion of the block going, to carry *uke*'s attacking arm back past his body. *Tori* then strikes across the throat

Spring hip throw (throw).

Back scoop ((i) initial balance take).

Back scoop ((i) throwing position).

Back scoop ((i) throw).

with his left forearm, taking hold of *uke*'s left shoulder with that hand, then pushing the forearm up and back against *uke*'s throat. This causes *uke* to arch back and allows *tori* to bring his right hand up between *uke*'s legs to grab the back of *uke*'s belt (in the street however a more obvious target would be grabbed if the opponent is male of course!). To complete the throw *tori* pivots *uke* about his mid-point by pulling back with his right hand (on the belt) and pushing forward with his left forearm (against the neck). *Tori* does not need to pick *uke* up, it is merely a pivoting motion. **(ii)** Following on logically the front scoop is the scoop that propels *uke* forwards. *Uke* attacks with a right punch to the face and *tori* parries with a right outside forearm parry while moving his left foot up level with *uke*'s right foot. *Tori* then strikes *uke* to the solar plexus. Shown here *tori* uses a right roundhouse kick but the choice of strike is dependent on the range to the target; at closer range it might be more appropriate to use a right knee or a right ridge hand strike. This strike should bend *uke* and *tori* then follows up with a right knife hand to *uke*'s medulla (the bump at the base of the skull just above the neck). *Tori* then reaches through *uke*'s legs and takes hold of the 'belt'. The throw is finished in one of two ways: *tori* can either pivot *uke* as with the back scoop (right hand forwards and left back), as shown here; or he can simply change his stance, moving his weight sharply forward onto his right leg, while pushing his right hand (and subsequently *uke*'s head) forwards and down into the floor.

8. Entangled Leg Lock

Tori begins by doing a leg throw (*see* Chapter 7) on the lead leg, in this case the right leg. He then kneels down on *uke*'s

Front scoop ((ii) initial take).

Front scoop ((ii) throw).

Entangled leg lock (initial strike after throw).

Entangled leg lock (taking the leg).

right side, level with *uke*'s hips, while keeping hold of *uke*'s leg with his right hand. *Tori* uses a left palm heel strike to *uke*'s groin, then with the same hand, grabs *uke*'s left ankle and pulls it up close to *uke*'s groin. Keeping his left hand where it is *tori* bends *uke*'s right leg until it comes to rest in front of his left leg (with the left ankle trapped against the inside of the right knee). *Tori* then brings his left hand under *uke*'s left leg and grabs hold of *uke*'s right ankle. To apply the lock *tori* pivots his left hand by raising his left elbow. If *uke* attempts to sit up this can be discouraged

Entangled leg lock (applying the lock).

Sleeper hold from headlock.

Restraining hold from headlock.

by use of *tori*'s left foot strategically placed on *uke*'s throat to pin him.

9. Sleeper Hold (and Restraining Hold) from Headlock

In both the sleeper hold and the restraining hold *uke* attacks with a right punch which *tori* parries with a left inside forearm parry. From there *tori* strikes the left side of *uke*'s neck with a right ridge hand then brings his right arm around *uke*'s neck (a headlock). In the sleeper hold *tori* places the bony end of his right radius bone (just above the thumb) in the hollow of *uke*'s right temple. *Tori* then places his left palm (palm up) on his right palm. To apply the lock *tori* pulls *uke*'s head into his body (directing his right wrist through *uke*'s temple and towards his body) and twists his hands slightly, so that his right thumb rises. If it is maintained for too long the hold will, as its name suggests, cause unconsciousness, so be careful.

The restraining hold is done in exactly the same way but the bony part of the radius is placed at the front of the muscle at *uke*'s right jaw joint. Application of the lock should cause pain, do not keep it on too long or the effectiveness will be reduced.

10. Outside Forearm Block, Elbow to Ribs

As with most of the techniques described this is only one representative technique; there are a host of possible variations. In this one *tori* blocks *uke* using a right outside forearm parry while moving his left foot up level with *uke*'s right foot. *Tori* then lowers his body and steps in with his right foot, striking *uke*'s ribs with his right elbow. Continuing the anticlockwise rotation of the body *tori* follows up with a left elbow to *uke*'s ribs. Turning back (clockwise) to stand behind *uke*, *tori* finishes by grabbing *uke*'s collar in his right hand (for collar also read hair, ears or whatever comes to hand) and, while pulling back on it, strikes the back of *uke*'s right knee with a right side thrust, pulling *uke* backwards and off balance.

11. Front Kick Followed by Side Kick

This is a practice of balance and combining different kicks. In this case *tori* is combining a right front snap kick and a side thrust kick. This is normally practised left- or right-footed and against either one or two opponents. The two kicks should be done using the same leg and without putting that leg down between the two moves. An important point is for *tori* to carefully pick his target and not just to kick blindly.

I have not shown them here as the individual kicks are described in Chapter 4. The only difference here is that the student must maintain balance and move straight to a second kick without placing his foot down (either against the same or a new opponent).

12. Three Blocks with the Same Arm

This is simply a practise with blocks. *Uke* attacks with a right punch to the face, a left to the face and a right to the body. *Tori* blocks with a right inside forearm parry, a left cross block and a left downwards inside forearm block.

Tori then changes to a right stance and blocks the same strikes using his right arm (right cross, right inside forearm, right downward inside forearm). See Chapter 3 for descriptions of the blocks.

Outside forearm block elbow to ribs (right elbow).

Outside forearm block elbow to ribs (left elbow).

Outside forearm block elbow to ribs (finish).

13. Attacks from Behind

Shown here are just four attacks. Although this looks aggressive and at odds with the 'self-defence' basis behind ju-jitsu there will be occasions where there is a need to act pre-emptively. An example being where you see someone being attacked and you move in to help them. It has been held up in court that a pre-emptive strike can be deemed self-defence but remember that you are the one that will have to justify it.

(i) First a simple double leg-take. *Tori* places his right foot between *uke*'s feet, takes hold of both *uke*'s ankles and leans his right shoulder into the back of *uke*'s legs. *Tori* then pushes forward with his shoulder while pulling back (and outwards) with his hands. The finish is a kick to the groin.

(ii) Here we see a single leg-take. *Tori* places his right leg through *uke*'s legs and in front of *uke*'s right, while at the same time taking hold of *uke*'s left ankle with his left hand and placing his right hand in the small of *uke*'s back. *Tori*'s right leg should be slightly bent (but with the back of it in close contact with the front of *uke*'s right

knee). To perform the technique *tori* pushes with his right arm (in the small of *uke*'s back) and pulls back on *uke*'s left leg while sharply straightening his right leg.

(iii) The third technique is the sweeping loin attack described in Chapter 7. To move in for the throw *tori* brings himself up alongside *uke*'s left and strikes backwards against *uke*'s left arm with his right. Snaking his right arm around *uke*'s waist *tori* now performs the sweeping loin as described.

(iv) Here *tori* takes hold of *uke*'s hair in his right hand, pulls backwards and uses a right-side thrust kick to the back of *uke*'s knee.

14. Transitional Hip Throw from a Double Block

Uke attacks with a right then a left punch to the face which *tori* defends using a left inside forearm parry then a left inside cross block. *Tori* then uses his left hand to strike the left-hand side of *uke*'s neck using a knife hand. *Tori* takes hold of *uke*'s neck with his left hand at the point of the strike and steps in with his right leg. *Tori* places

Attack from behind ((i) double leg take).

Attack from behind ((ii) single leg take).

Attack from behind ((iii) a, sweeping loin).

Attack from behind ((iii) b, sweeping loin).

Attack from behind ((iv) hair grab and kick).

Transitional hip throw (second block).

Transitional hip throw (neck take).

Transitional hip throw (throw).

his right foot just on the inside of *uke's* right foot and puts his right arm around *uke's* waist. *Tori* then brings his left leg up until it is just on the inside of *uke's* left foot. The feet and body are virtually identical to a hip throw (*see* Chapter 5), the differences are the position of the left hand on *uke's* neck and its subsequent use to pull *uke* around (replacing the use of *uke's* right arm) and that *tori* does not put his hip quite as far through as for the hip throw.

Note: for *uke's* safety when doing this throw *uke* needs to place his right arm around the front of *tori's* stomach. This allows *uke* to achieve a proper break-fall and prevents him from breaking his right wrist or arm by putting it out in front of him when he is thrown.

15. Variations of Hold-downs and Ground Locks

Here we are looking at a few of the main locks and holds used in ju-jitsu. For ease of demonstration I have shown these as a sequence one after the other.

(i) The first lock shown is the 'cricket bat' lock (the reason for the name should be obvious). After *uke* has been thrown to the ground *tori* retains hold of his right arm (from a right-hand throw) at the wrist with his left hand. *Tori* pulls upwards on the arm and twists *uke's* wrist so that the back of *uke's* elbow is facing towards him. *Tori* then slides his right hand down the forearm and pushes forward whilst bringing his right knee down just behind *uke's* ear. Please note that *tori's* right hand has the thumb on the right of *uke's* arm and pointing down (as if one were holding a cricket bat in fact).

(ii) and (iii) The second lock is the cross-arm lock shown in Chapter 6. From this lock *tori* places his left arm across the inside of *uke's* elbow joint (so that the thinnest part of *tori's* forearm is across the joint). *Tori* then takes hold of *uke's* hand (right in this case) with his right so that his palm is on the back of *uke's* hand and *tori's* thumb is facing down *uke's* arm. *Tori* bends *uke's* arm and takes hold of his own right wrist with his left hand. From here *tori* leans back to apply the lock.

(iv) The next lock follows on by *tori* coming forward so that his left leg, which is already across *uke's* neck, wraps around *uke's* neck completely. The armlock is simply applied by placing the back of *uke's* right elbow against *tori's* knee and pulling back on his wrist (note that pressure can also be applied to the neck at this point).

(v) The next lock is the double armlock hold-down shown in Chapter 7.

(vi) For the hold shown *uke's* right arm is pushed right across his face and *tori* slides his right arm underneath *uke's* neck. Linking his hands palm to palm *tori* can apply pressure by pulling both of his hands towards him and twisting upwards. This causes the bony part of *tori's* right wrist (see the ridge hand in Chapter 2) to grind into the back of *uke's* neck.

(vii) The final lock is where *uke* is face down. *Tori* takes hold of *uke's* right hand with his right hand so that his palm is on the back of *uke's* hand; his fingers have hold of the meat of *uke's* palm by the little finger and his thumb is on the back of the hand. Twisting *uke's* hand so that the fingers are facing up *tori* pushes down on *uke's* shoulder with his left hand and pushes *uke's* straight arm anticlockwise (as if the arm were the minute hand of a clock centred at the shoulder). It is important to keep the arm straight and touching the floor throughout.

Shoulder dislocations could also be included here, *see* Chapter 10 for descriptions.

Variation of hold-down and ground lock (i).

Variation of hold-down and ground lock (ii).

Variation of hold-down and ground lock (iii).

Variation of hold-down and ground lock (iv).

16. Advanced Breaking of Ground Strangles

These escapes follow on from the yellow belt escapes and become a little more involved. I have shown a few here for examples but as you can imagine there are many more.

(i) This first break involves an attacker coming from between *tori*'s legs, on the ground, into a straight strangle. *Tori* uses a weakener (a strike to the ribs or solar plexus) then takes hold of *uke*'s wrists and

Variation of hold-down and ground lock (v).

Advanced breaking of ground strangles ((i) initial foot placement).

Advanced breaking of ground strangles ((i) finish).

Advanced breaking of ground strangles ((ii) taking wrist and leg).

Advanced breaking of ground strangles ((ii) applying lock).

places his heels inside the crease between *uke*'s thighs and hips. *Tori* then simultaneously pushes with his legs and breaks *uke*'s grip on his neck. As *tori* is using his leg muscles to break a handhold this should not be too difficult. You will find that depending on the relative size of *uke* and *tori* either one or both will move; this is not a problem as what *tori* is aiming for is to increase the gap between them. This gap should be large enough for *tori* to introduce *uke*'s head (nicely placed) to his foot.

(ii) This second escape is from the same attack. *Tori* again performs a weakener then brings his right hand underneath *uke*'s left arm, coming up between *uke*'s arms to take hold of *uke*'s right hand with his fingers underneath the hand (in the palm) and his thumb on the back. At the same time *tori* brings his right foot over *uke*'s left leg, placing his foot on the floor between *uke*'s legs, and then slides it to the right so that it hooks underneath *uke*'s left ankle. *Tori* then straightens his right leg sharply and twists *uke*'s right wrist

Advanced breaking of ground strangles ((iii) take wrist and knee strike).

Advanced breaking of ground strangles ((iii) leg over neck).

clockwise and off to the right. From here *tori* can finish the lock, strike *uke*'s unprotected side or get to his feet (or a combination of all three).

(iii) The third escape shown is from a side strangle, again on the ground. *Tori* takes hold of *uke*'s left wrist with both hands and brings both legs straight up towards *uke*. *Tori*'s left knee strikes *uke* in the rib cage while *tori*'s right leg wraps around *uke*'s neck. *Tori* then straightens his right leg, bringing *uke* down to the floor, and applies a cross-arm lock (*see* Chapter 6).

Advanced breaking of ground strangles ((iii) lock).

10 Purple Belt

1. Counters to Straight-Arm Lock

Here *tori* is countering the straight-arm lock described in Chapter 5. It is the nature of combat that for every technique there is a countermove and for every countermove a 'counter-countermove'. True combat is all about the flow between technique and counter-technique, the winner is the one who doesn't make a mistake (or more realistically, who makes the smallest mistake). If the initial technique is done correctly there can be no counter; the counter introduces aspects designed to disrupt the initial technique and to allow for the counter-technique to take place. In this case the aspects introduced are to prevent the elbow strike to the face at the start of the straight-arm lock and to rotate the attacked arm slightly to prevent any lock from being applied.

(i) As mentioned *uke* attacks using a straight-arm lock (*tori* therefore initiated in practice with a punch to *uke*'s stomach) on *tori*'s right arm. *Tori* blocks the elbow to the face with his left hand and turns his right hand so that the palm is facing downwards. This turn of the palm is enough to stop the lock going on straight away. *Tori* then pushes *uke*'s left (striking) elbow away from him using his left hand while at the same time bringing his right hand downwards and back against the inside of *uke*'s left forearm. By pushing down on *uke*'s elbow with his left hand and bringing

his right hand up *tori* can straighten *uke*'s left arm and apply a counter-lock. To apply the lock *tori* keeps his left hand on *uke*'s elbow and his right forearm underneath *uke*'s forearm. *Tori* moves so that *uke*'s hand comes up under his armpit and then *tori* places his right hand on his left forearm. This should be recognizable by now as a 'figure-four' variety of armlock and is applied by slowly straightening the arms.

(ii) In this second counter *tori* stops the lock as before but this time pulls *uke*'s left elbow across in front of his chest, pushing his right arm up into *uke*'s armpit (using his right arm in the same way as for a one-arm shoulder throw, *see* Chapter 7). *Tori* then extends his right leg out in front of *uke*'s legs and throws *uke* with a variation of a body drop shoulder throw (*see* Chapter 8 for the body drop shoulder throw, the variation is that *tori* is performing a right-handed throw but is using *uke*'s left arm. See later in the chapter for more of these types of throw.). As with the transitional hip throw in training it is in *uke*'s best interest to wrap his right arm around *tori*'s stomach to allow for a break-fall (and no broken arm or wrist!).

(iii) Starting with the block *tori* then places his right leg behind *uke* while at the same time bending his right arm (at a ninety-degree angle) and striking *uke* to the groin. *Tori* then drops his weight slightly and propels *uke* backwards over his leg using his right elbow. This can

Counter to straight-arm lock ((i) block elbow and turn wrist).

Counter to straight-arm lock ((i) draw uke's arm back).

Counter to straight-arm lock ((i) lock).

Counter to straight-arm lock ((ii) arm position).

Counter to straight-arm lock ((ii) throw position).

Counter to straight-arm lock ((ii) throw).

Counter to straight-arm lock ((iii) strike).

either be done standing (as shown in escapes from bear hugs (iv) in Chapter 8) or as a sacrifice throw by falling backwards with *uke*. The sacrifice throw is, as already mentioned, a last resort and should only be used in reality where the difference in size between *tori* and *uke* exceeds *tori*'s skill with the non-sacrificial version (strength is not an issue, just skill: the better you are at a technique the less *uke*'s size matters).

2. Counters to Arm and Collar Hold

First a description of the hold and the immediate response needed from *tori* in all cases: the hold involves *uke* taking hold of *tori*'s right wrist with his right hand, bending *tori*'s arm behind his back and taking hold of *tori*'s collar with his left

hand (and vice versa for a left-handed version). *Tori*'s immediate response to this must be to arch his spine, preventing his arm from being pushed right up his back. He can then respond with one of the following:

(i) From this position *tori* turns to his left, opening up *uke*'s body as a target area, and strikes either with a left elbow to *uke*'s solar plexus or a left knife hand to *uke*'s floating ribs. As he is doing this *tori* needs to grab *uke*'s right wrist with his right hand. *Tori* then turns back clockwise and brings his right elbow up to strike the right-hand side of *uke*'s face. Having kept hold of *uke*'s right wrist *uke*'s arm should now be in an upright L-shape. From here *tori* brings his left arm up behind *uke*'s upper right arm, and through the gap, to grasp the front of his own right wrist, thus applying a figure-four armlock (*see* Chapter 6).

(ii) As for (i) *tori* starts with a turn to the left and a strike to *uke*'s ribs or solar plexus while taking hold of *uke*'s right wrist with his right hand. From there *tori* turns clockwise and places his left foot further forward in front of his right (directly ahead as *uke* sees it). *Tori* turns their body further clockwise and brings his now straightened right arm upwards, making a vertical clockwise circle with his (and subsequently *uke*'s) right hand. As he brings his right hand down *tori* draws it towards himself, bringing *uke* off balance, and steps back further with his right leg (past his left foot), pulling all the while. This brings him alongside the outside of *uke*'s right arm. As long as *tori* has been pulling steadily (this is obviously better at some speed) *uke*'s right arm should now be horizontal in front of him and all *tori* needs to do is place his left hand on the back of *uke*'s right elbow to apply a straight-arm bar, taking him to the floor if desired.

Counter to arm and collar hold ((i) first strike).

Counter to arm and collar hold ((i) second strike).

Counter to arm and collar hold ((i) lock).

Counter to arm and collar hold ((ii) stepping out).

(iii) Here we start with the turn and strike as before but this time *tori* continues moving anticlockwise. After striking with the left hand *tori* uses this to protect his face (from *uke*'s right knee) as he continues the turn, coming out and up under *uke*'s right arm. As he starts to come upright *tori* brings *uke*'s right arm up behind *uke*'s back in a figure-four shape. From here *tori* can bring his left hand up through the gap formed in the middle of *tori* and *uke*'s right arms and grasp his right wrist to form a reversed figure-four armlock (this could also be referred to as a reinforced entangled armlock).

Counter to arm and collar hold ((ii) lock).

Counter to arm and collar hold ((iii) duck under).

Counter to arm and collar hold ((iii) lock).

Roundhouse kicks to kidneys (regular roundhouse).

Roundhouse kicks to kidneys (back heel).

3. Roundhouse Kicks to the Kidneys

This is a simple defence from a punch to the face using a roundhouse kick and a roundhouse back heel. Owing to the similarities I have only included one basic roundhouse and one back heel.

(i) Using a left inside forearm parry *tori* leans backwards and kicks to *uke*'s kidneys with his left leg.

(ii) Here *tori* uses exactly the same kick but this time uses a left outside forearm parry.

(iii) From a right stance (but still defending from a right punch) *tori* uses a right cross block, leans back onto the left leg and brings the right heel into *uke*'s kidney (a clockwise sweep of the right leg).

(iv) This time *tori* uses a right-hand outside forearm parry but performs the same back heel kick as for (iii).

Two upwards blocks followed with strike (second block).

Two upwards blocks followed with strike (strike).

Full shoulder throw (strike).

Full shoulder throw (throw position).

4. Two Upwards Blocks Followed with a Strike

For this technique *uke* attacks with a right punch to the face followed by a left, also to the face. *Tori* uses a left upwards inside forearm block (also called a left upwards rising block, *see* Chapter 3). *Tori* takes hold of *uke*'s right arm with his left hand and pulls him forwards and down to the left (*tori*'s left). If done correctly this should have the effect of reducing the effectiveness of *uke*'s left punch, which *tori* then blocks with a right upwards rising block. *Tori* then performs a strike of his choice.

5. Full Shoulder Throw

Uke attacks with a right punch to the face and *tori* defends using a left upward rising block. Stepping in with the right foot, placing it just in front of *uke*'s, *tori* strikes up into the hollow of *uke*'s armpit with a right leopard punch (be very careful of this strike in practise as any strike to the lymph glands can be painful!). *Tori* then turns in, bringing his left foot up level with his right, a shoulder width apart (the turn in for this throw brings *tori*'s backside onto *uke*'s right thigh, slightly further out than for a hip throw), knees bent. As they are turning in *tori* brings *uke*'s right arm to rest on his right shoulder and takes hold with his right hand high up on *uke*'s right arm. When done in self-defence *tori* would have turned *uke*'s right arm so that the elbow is facing down and the palm up; don't try the throw this way in practise but do try the lock so that you know how it works. From here *tori* pulls *uke* straight forward while straightening his legs and, if possible, skipping backwards slightly as he does so. When doing this throw it is helpful to raise your right shoulder slightly, to prevent *uke*'s arm from sliding off.

6. Reverse Full Shoulder

This throw is very similar to the full shoulder in the mechanics of the throw. This time however *tori* uses a right outside forearm parry and a left punch to the ribs. From the outside of *uke*'s right arm *tori* steps through with his left foot placing his feet and hips in the same position as for

Reverse full shoulder.

the full shoulder. For this throw however *tori* has *uke*'s right arm on top of his left shoulder (with the left shoulder raised slightly). From here the throw is performed as for the full shoulder.

7. Neck Winding Throw

Parrying a right punch to the face with a left inside forearm parry *tori* takes hold of *uke*'s right hand with his left. *Tori* then strikes the left hand side of *uke*'s neck with a ridge hand strike. From here *tori* slides his right arm around *uke*'s neck as far as he can while at the same time turning his hip in as for previous hip throws. The hip position should be further through than that for a normal hip throw, almost as far through as for the loin/hip wheel. Note that the positions of the feet at this stage are the same as for a hip throw.

Keeping a tight hold on *uke*'s neck *tori* kneels down on his right knee. As with the dropping version of a full shoulder (*see* Chapter 8) it is important for *tori* to slide his right foot outwards and place his knee in the space that the foot vacates. As *tori* is kneeling down he needs to turn his hips further through and draw his arms (and subsequently *uke*'s right arm and head!) across the front of his body in a right-to-left motion.

8. Inner and Outer Winding Throws

The movements for these two throws are so similar that I will describe them together. From a right punch *tori* uses a right inside forearm parry and takes hold of *uke*'s right arm with his left hand. *Tori* steps in with his right foot to just in front of *uke*'s right foot and strikes. For the inner winding *tori* strikes with either the right palm heel or elbow to *uke*'s floating ribs and in the case of the outer winding they use a right palm heel to *uke*'s jaw. Continuing this rotation *tori* brings his left foot round and turns his hips through (as for the neck winding throw). For the inner *tori* pulls *uke*'s arm tight so that the side of *tori*'s shoulder is tight up against the underneath and inside of *uke*'s shoulder. For the outer *uke*'s shoulder needs to be pulled tight into *tori*'s armpit. Keeping *uke*'s right arm tight across his chest (no gaps) *tori* now finishes as for the neck winding throw by turning the hips further in, moving his right foot out and placing his right knee where it was, and drawing both hands down to his left hip. There is a nastier variation of both involving a sweep, but I'm not going to describe that here. The first two pictures here just show the outer winding throw and the last one shows the throw position for inner winding.

Neck winding throw (strike).

Neck winding throw (wind).

9. Wedge Block with Throw

This technique is performed from a grappling position with *uke* grabbing *tori*'s lapels. *Tori* brings his hands up under *uke*'s arms to in turn grab *uke*'s lapels. From here *tori* lifts his elbows under *uke*'s arms. This weakens *uke*'s position, so that they bring less force to bear on *tori*. *Tori* adjusts his balance so that his rear leg is taking the force of *uke*'s push, thus allowing him to kick with his front leg.

After the kick *uke* is open to numerous throws and which one is *tori*'s decision. (The kick however is optional as after the initial movements (grab and elbow raise) *tori* is in a perfect position to perform many of the sacrificial techniques described throughout the book, two obvious ones being the rolling ankle and the corner throw which are described later on in this chapter.)

Neck winding throw (throw).

Outer winding throw (throw position).

Outer winding throw (throw).

Inner winding throw (throw position).

Wedge block.

10. Valley Drop Throw

This throw comes under the heading of a sacrifice throw and, as its name suggests, *tori* sacrifices his position to make it work. As such all sacrifice throws should only be done where other options are not available, particularly if *uke* is not alone! The second point with all sacrifice throws is that once it is done, get yourself off the floor (fast!).

The valley drop is normally practised from a grappling position, with *uke* taking hold of *tori*'s shoulders and pushing forward. *Tori* takes hold of *uke*'s right arm up near the shoulder and his left arm under the armpit. *Tori* then places both feet together just outside *uke*'s right foot. From here *tori* allows his body to fall across the front of *uke*'s feet (the nearer the better: try to land on both of *uke*'s feet) and at the same time he rolls his body away from *uke*, extending his arms. So long as this is done while *uke* is pushing against you, *uke* will fly over you. If *tori* keeps hold with his left hand this encourages *uke* to land on his back. *Tori* can then finish rolling in that

Valley drop throw (throw position).

Valley drop throw (throw).

Rolling ankle throw (falling position).

Rolling ankle throw (throw).

direction and give *uke* a right kick before getting to his feet. This description and pictures are for a right-handed valley drop which is used when *uke* has his right foot forward; if he has his left leg forward simply reverse the technique.

11. Rolling Ankle Throw

As mentioned earlier this can be done from a wedge block if you wish; I prefer taking hold of *uke*'s right arm and left lapel (and vice versa for the other side). The side on which you perform this throw is decided by *uke*'s foot position; you will always utilize the front foot. In this case *uke* has his right foot forward therefore *tori* places his left foot on *uke*'s right foot, at the ankle joint. *Tori* then drops his weight to his right, sitting down just past his own right foot. Removing himself from the front of *uke* and pulling *uke* forward *tori* pulls *uke* sharply off balance. As his front foot is pinned *uke* cannot move it to regain his balance and will fall forwards. As he does so *tori* 'assists' his fall by pulling his left arm into his body, pushing outwards (forwards as *uke* looks at it) with his right

111

Corner throw (initial position).

Corner throw (throw).

arm and pushing upwards with his right foot. In the training hall *uke* will do a rolling break-fall and in the street *uke* will land in a dishevelled heap. In both cases *tori* gets to his feet as soon as he can; as I mentioned already this is true for all sacrifice throws.

For the throw to work properly *uke* must be committed to pushing *tori*, thus propelling his balance forward. *Tori* can induce this by pushing *uke* backwards; this causes *uke* to naturally want to push against *tori*.

12. Corner Throw

This has a similar start to the rolling ankle throw, starting in the grapple position. For this throw *tori* brings his right foot across to *uke*'s right (or left to left). *Tori* places his right foot on the outside of *uke*'s right foot and bends his knee inwards; this will push on the inside of *uke*'s knee causing it to buckle. As with the rolling ankle *tori* now drops his weight down and to his right removing himself from *uke*'s front. As he drops down *tori* pulls in with his left arm, pushes with his right and flicks upwards with his right leg. Finish off as per the rolling ankle.

13. Rear Throw

This technique can be done either defensively from a punch or as an attack from behind. In case you are wondering why an art used for defence should need techniques such as attacks from behind, first consider the old truism that 'attack is the best form of defence' (a pre-emptive strike in modern terms) and second what *uke* might be doing that requires you to take action (threatening a friend for example; use your imagination).

The only difference between the two is the start, the first starts with an inside forearm parry from which *tori* does three things almost simultaneously. *Tori* strikes the back of *uke*'s neck with the palm of his blocking hand, brings both feet to the side of *uke*'s (on the same side as the blocking hand) and then strikes *uke*'s stomach with the palm heel of his non-blocking hand. As he strikes the stomach *tori*'s body needs to be falling across *uke*'s front (with the feeling of trying to land on *uke*'s feet), pulling with the hand behind the neck and pushing with the hand in the stomach. Finish off as per the last two techniques.

For the second the only difference is that coming from behind *uke*, on either

Rear throw (initial position).

Rear throw (throw).

Variation of leg sweep ((i) sweeping the lower shin).

Variation of leg sweep ((ii) regular).

side, you strike the back of his neck with the palm of the nearest hand then turn to strike the stomach with the other hand as you fall across the front of *uke*.

14. Variations of Leg Sweeps

This is included to encourage the student to adapt their technique to the situation and the person. It shows several variations of the basic sweeping loin throw from Chapter 7 (although some of the variations

Variation of leg sweep ((iii) sweeping the knee).

Variation of leg sweep ((iv) sweeping the thigh).

Variation of leg sweep ((v) rear sweep).

are different enough from the original to warrant being separate throws in their own right). For (i) to (iv) the throw is done identically to the sweeping loin except for the position of the sweeping leg.

(i) The sweep is on the shin, with the heel hitting the lower shin.
(ii) This is the traditional sweeping loin, sweeping with *tori*'s calf mid way up *uke*'s shin.
(iii) *Tori* sweeps *uke*'s knee.
(iv) *Tori* sweeps at mid-thigh level (slightly lower than the leg wheel with different positioning and balance, *see* Chapter 11).
(v) This last one is different in that the technique is started in the same way as an outer reaping throw (*see* Chapter 7) but instead of taking the nearest leg *tori* takes both (again this is different from the similar-looking outer wheel, *see* Chapter 11).

15. Shoulder Wheel

This throw, when done correctly, requires little or no effort to perform; when it is done wrongly it is a case of brute force over ignorance! *Tori* uses a standard inside

forearm parry with his left and takes hold of *uke*'s arm. *Tori* then steps in and places his right foot next to the inside of *uke*'s right foot while drawing *uke*'s right arm upwards and forwards (as seen by *uke*). At the same time *tori* bends his right leg and places his right arm along the front of *uke*'s right shin with the hand taking hold at the ankle. *Tori* then straightens his left arm causing *uke*'s right arm to be extended further, bringing *uke* across *tori*'s shoulders. *Tori* should now have *uke* extended across his shoulders. *Tori*'s right leg should be bent and his left leg straight. To perform the throw *tori* keeps himself at the same height but changes his stance. All of *tori*'s weight needs to be shifted to his left leg by straightening the right and bending the left. At the same time *tori* brings his left arm down and raises his right (with both arms extended).

This means that *tori* starts with: right leg bent; right hand down; left leg straight; left arm high, and moves to: right leg straight; right hand high; left leg bent; and left arm low.

This change of stance, when done correctly, is what makes the throw virtually effortless. It can be done by getting *uke* onto your shoulders then standing up to complete the throw but my opinion is that this wastes valuable time and energy.

16. Outer Hook Throw

As demonstrated here this would best be described as a leg trap rather than a leg sweep. *Tori* uses a left inside forearm parry and in preparation brings his right foot up close to his lead foot. *Tori* uses the blocking arm to strike the left side of *uke*'s neck with a knife hand while at the same time pinning *uke*'s right leg with his left. *Tori*'s left leg should be bent around and tight up against *uke*'s leg with the heel off the floor. The technique is completed by *tori* stamping his left heel down, straightening the left leg and allowing the strike to *uke*'s neck to carry on backwards and to the left.

17. Shoulder Dislocations

All of the dislocations here are shown with a prone *uke* for clarity (I am sure you will find plenty in this book to put *uke* into this lamentable position).

(i) With his knees either side of *uke*, *tori* takes hold of both of *uke*'s hands and turns them so that *uke*'s palms are facing towards his own head. With *tori*'s fingers curled into *uke*'s palms and his thumbs on the back of *uke*'s hand (thumb facing up with the meaty pad at the base of the thumb positioned in the middle of the back of *uke*'s hand) *tori* applies the dislocation by pushing his hands straight forwards.
(ii) This is completed as per (i) but to apply more force *tori* stands up.
(iii) Following on from (ii) where more force or forward motion is needed (with either a very strong a very flexible *uke*) *tori*

Shoulder wheel (initial position).

Shoulder wheel (throw).

Outer hook throw (initial position).

Shoulder dislocation (i).

Shoulder dislocation (ii).

Shoulder dislocation (iii).

steps forward with one foot. Keeping *uke*'s arms parallel with his body *tori* is able to bring all of his body weight to bear on *uke*'s unfortunate shoulder joints.

(iv) For this dislocation *tori* pins *uke*'s right shoulder with his left hand (using his body weight down through his arm) and takes hold of *uke*'s right hand with his own right. *Tori* should have the fingers of *uke*'s hand pointing away and *uke*'s palm facing his own head (tori should be gripping the hand with his palm on the back of *uke*'s hand and his hand at a right angle to *uke*'s). The lock is put on by rotating *uke*'s arm in a big circle, anticlockwise, while keeping the arm straight and on the floor.

(v) For this lock *tori* has the same grip as (iv) but pins the shoulder with his left knee and pushes *uke*'s arm diagonally forward and to the left.

Shoulder dislocation (iv).

Shoulder dislocation (v).

Shoulder dislocation (vi).

Snap kick to knee (upwards and inwards).

(vi) From (v) if *tori* now steps over *uke*'s arm with his left leg and bends *uke*'s arm back to sit against their left hip they can lower themselves down into the lock shown. This is a very powerful hold and to apply the lock simply lift the backside up and lean forward.

18. Side Snap Kicks and Upward Kicks to the Knee

The side snap kicks are performed in the same way as the front snap kicks but with a turn of the hips that rotates the striking

Snap kick to knee (upwards and outwards).

foot to hit side-on (*see* Chapter 4 for a more detailed description). The two shown here are by way of example but the range is varied.

19. Left Punch Throws

The basic premise behind this range of techniques is that *tori* has used an inside forearm parry in defending himself against a right punch to the face but is instead receiving a left punch to the face. As described before the inside forearm parry, when performed correctly, will become an outside forearm parry if *uke* uses the opposite arm in attacking. This set of techniques is an exercise in adapting ordinary throws to this unusual position. Obviously if *tori* has blocked the inside of *uke*'s left punch then the techniques can just be done left-handed but from the outside of *uke*'s left arm (again equally applicable to the outside of *uke*'s right arm) the ordinary throws can still be done. The three shown here are the hip throw (*see* Chapter 5), the body drop (*see* Chapter 6) and the one-arm shoulder throw (*see* Chapter 7).

Left punch throw (hip throw).

Left punch throw (one-armed shoulder throw).

Left punch throw (body drop).

11 Brown Belt

1. Palm Heel Blocks with Strikes (following on from Chapter 3)

Palm heel blocks are no more, or less, than the use of the heel of the palm as the blocking surface. As part of this the palm heel block is also a strike. Because of the nature of these blocks they are in equal measures a more effective block and a more difficult block to perform correctly. There are two ways to perform the palm heel block: the first (which I find far more effective) is to block with the fingers of *tori*'s blocking arm pointing along *uke*'s arm or leg towards his foot or hand; the second is for *tori* to align his hand so that his fingers are at a right angle to *uke*'s limb. The former uses a circular motion and the latter a straight action.

The exact target area for each block is varied and will change with each combat situation but I have put here a few examples of 'sweet' points for three different circumstances. When blocking to the outside of *uke*'s attacking arm (shown here as the right arm) *tori* here steps with his left foot forward and to the left slightly and strikes to *uke*'s elbow with his left palm heel (finishing with a right punch to the face). When blocking on the inside of *uke*'s arm (again here the right) *tori* steps in with the right foot and strikes with his right palm heel to the inside of *uke*'s forearm. (In this case the exact target is approximately one-quarter of the way down the forearm as measured from the elbow; as well as being the most effective position for this block from a mechanical point of view there is

Palm heel block (outer arm).

Palm heel block (inner arm).

Palm heel block (knee).

Cross ankle throw (initial kick).

Cross ankle throw (throw position).

also a neat bundle of nerve endings at this point that does interesting things when struck.) To use a palm heel block against a front snap kick uses the same principle but the target for the block is the kneecap. If using the left hand to block *tori* steps forward and to the left slightly, with his left foot, and blocks downwards with the left palm heel (just reverse this to block with the right). This works with a left or right attack. As mentioned I prefer to have the fingers pointing along the limb: in the case of this last block you strike using the palm heel with the feeling of aiming *uke*'s kneecap towards his feet, thus at best *uke* will greatly overreach himself (and at worst, for *uke*, you succeed!).

2. Cross Ankle Throw

At first glance this throw bears a great resemblance to the body drop (in Chapter 6), there are significant differences however. The initial block uses an inside forearm parry taking hold of the attacking arm, combined with a left kick to *uke*'s left kneecap. The kicking foot is then placed on the outside of *uke*'s left foot. *Tori* pivots on his left foot in an anticlockwise direction and places his right leg across the front of *uke*'s legs. This is where the main differences lie. *Tori*'s right foot is placed just outside *uke*'s right foot, meaning that the pivot point on *uke* and *tori* is their right ankle, and as part of the rotation that places their foot there *tori* brings his right arm (straight and rigid) up under *uke*'s left armpit. *Tori* continues the anticlockwise rotation with his arms and upper body, bringing his right arm around to the front in a sweeping arc. Note that the pivot point is different from that of a body drop (where it is *tori*'s knee), as is the contact point for the right arm. Once *tori* starts to pivot he needs to continue in one flowing motion; arresting the flow at any point makes the throw very difficult to perform. This throw shows one end of a spectrum of throws that starts with the body drop. They all use similar mechanics but vary in *tori*'s position relative to *uke*. This is meant to show that there aren't just the two throws but a whole range depending on your position; combat is fluid and your body has to learn to react to this with the correct mechanics of motion.

3. Leg Wheel

As with the previous throw this technique

Leg wheel (throw position).

Leg wheel (throw).

Outer wheel (throw position).

Outer wheel (throw).

is not to be seen as a throw on its own but as one end of a spectrum of throws starting with sweeping loin (*see* Chapter 7). With this throw *tori* finds himself further to the side of *uke*'s body and due to his position wheels him over the leg rather than attempting to sweep the leg. From an inside forearm parry *tori* kicks *uke*'s left knee with his left foot and steps to just outside *uke*'s left foot (as with the previous throw). Pivoting this time *tori* places his right arm around *uke*'s waist then turns anticlockwise and brings *uke* close to his right hip, tilting away from *uke* to put the weight over his left leg and bring *uke* off

balance. *Tori* then swings his right leg upwards and slightly back whilst pulling *uke* forward (and around) using the arm and the hand around *uke*'s waist. The leg over which *uke* is wheeled remains straight: to do this it helps to point the toes down and the heel up when swinging it upwards.

4. Outer Wheel

The outer wheel is very similar in application to the leg wheel, only the direction that *uke* faces is different. Here *tori* blocks a right punch with a left inside forearm

Stomach throw ((i) side, foot position).

Stomach throw ((i) side, throw).

block, stepping forward as he blocks so that his left foot is level with the outside of *uke*'s right foot (as with the outer reaping throw in Chapter 7). *Tori* brings his right ridge hand up to strike the left side of *uke*'s neck, while at the same time leaning to put his weight over his left foot. At this stage *tori* should have his right hip in contact with *uke*'s right hip. Keeping his right hip in contact with *uke*, *tori* brings his right leg up behind *uke*'s legs and sweeps his right leg upwards and slightly back (as with the previous technique) and pulls around in an anticlockwise motion with both arms (using a twist in the torso to help this along).

5. Stomach Throws

Here we are looking at the most recognizable of the sacrifice throws. I have shown three basic variations here: side, basic and double leg. These throws can be performed either from a defence against a punch or from a grapple position; I have just described the mechanics of the throw itself.

(i) The side throw (left or right) is different from the other two in that it causes *uke* to rotate in two different planes at once.

Once *tori* has a grip on *uke*, normally upper arm and lapel (but be flexible), he brings one of his feet up and places it in the crease between *uke*'s lower abdomen and his leg. Here we have shown *tori* bringing up his right foot and placing it on the left side of *uke*'s body. The toes should be pointing up and out, the heel facing down and inwards. From here *tori* bends his supporting leg and places his backside on the floor under his raised foot, as near to *uke*'s feet as possible. This means in the throw shown that *tori* is moving his centre of gravity from the middle of *uke* to *uke*'s left side. As he is doing this *tori* pulls *uke* forward and straightens his raised leg. This means that *uke* falls forwards (one plane) while their body is rotating away to *tori*'s side (in this case rotating anticlockwise and towards *tori*'s left side).

(ii) This second stomach throw is the more commonly recognizable. Once *tori* has hold of *uke* he plants his right foot (or left) on *uke*'s stomach, leg bent. He bends his supporting leg bringing his backside to the floor central to *uke* and as near to *uke*'s feet as possible. While doing this *tori* pulls *uke* forwards using his body weight. Once his backside is on the floor, and *uke* is falling (but not before), *tori* continues

Stomach throw ((ii) front, foot position).

Stomach throw ((ii) front, throw).

Stomach throw ((iii) double leg, secondary foot position).

Stomach throw ((iii) double, throw).

rolling backwards pulling *uke*'s upper body forward and down (aiming to put *uke*'s face on the ground just above his own head). Once *uke*'s body is directly over *tori*'s, *tori* straightens his right leg, pushing it towards his own head. This then propels *uke* over and away from *tori*.

(iii) This throw starts identically to the side stomach throw (i), with *tori* placing one foot to the side of *uke*'s abdomen. The difference comes when *tori*'s back is on the floor; at this point he raises his other foot and places it in the corresponding position on the other side of *uke*'s abdomen. *Tori* continues rolling backwards then, when

uke is directly over him, *tori* straightens both legs backwards over his own head. Ideally the second foot will connect with *uke*'s abdomen at the same point that *tori* would have begun straightening his leg in the first two throws. It is important to remember that the second foot is brought up after *tori*'s back is on the floor. If *tori* brings his second foot off the floor too early then there is no control over the speed at which his back will hit the floor. In reality, on stone or concrete, this would result in serious back injury. This is training designed for defeating an opponent in real combat, it is not American wrestling!

Defence against attack from the rear
(neck and arm held).

Defence against attack from the rear
(neck and arm defence).

Defence against attack from the rear
(over-and-under bear hug).

Defence against attack from the rear
(over-and-under defence).

Defence against attack from the rear
(double-linked arms).

Defence against attack from the rear
(double-linked defence).

6. Defences against Attacks from the Rear

This is to test the student's ability to think on their feet and use any number of the escapes they have learned up to this point. It also tests their ability to improvise using the whole range of their skills. Here I have shown a defence from a neck lock with the arm held, a defence from an over-and-under bear hug and a defence from a double-linked arm hold. Although none of these holds have been specifically covered in the book you should be able (if you have studied properly to get to this level) to spot where the defences come from. All it needs is a little improvisation and adaptation.

7. Shoulder Crash

While a very similar throw to the shoulder wheel, the effect of this technique is considerably more devastating. The initial part of the throw is the same as for shoulder wheel (*see* Chapter 10). *Tori* uses an inside forearm parry with his left arm, takes hold of *uke*'s right arm (just swap left for right and vice versa for the left-handed version), and then places his right foot in next to *uke*'s right while drawing *uke*'s attacking arm forwards (as *uke* sees it) to pull him off balance. *Tori* then bends underneath *uke*'s point of balance and shifts his balance forwards so that his right shoulder is in contact with *uke*'s leg, placing his right hand on the front of *uke*'s shin. Keeping tight contact with *uke*'s body, and keeping his own left arm extended straight out, *tori* shifts his weight back over to his left side, bringing *uke*'s body up onto his shoulders. This is where the technique varies from the shoulder wheel; *tori* now straightens his legs quickly while at the same time allowing his feet to skip backwards slightly. This should bring *uke*'s body in front of *tori* at which point *tori* propels *uke* into the floor. In training it is necessary to rotate *uke* slightly as you are propelling him thus allowing him to break-fall.

Shoulder crash (initial position).

Shoulder crash (throw).

Palm heel knockout blow ((i) non-blocking hand).

Palm heel knockout blow ((ii) blocking hand).

Palm heel knockout blow ((iii) upwards).

Palm heel knockout blow ((iii) following elbow).

8. Palm Heel Knockout Blows

For information about the reasons for and the effectiveness of palm heel strikes *see* Chapter 2.

(i) For this first strike *tori* uses the non-blocking hand and strikes with the fingers in a horizontal position. The striking point is just in front of *uke*'s left jaw hinge point. The motion of the strike is through *uke*'s head, right to left (as seen by *tori*), but with a curve in the path, with *tori* as the centre of the curvature.

(ii) The second palm heel strike uses the blocking hand but the strike point and motion are the same as for (i) (although in opposite directions). With both these strikes *tori* rotates his upper body to add to the force of the blow.

(iii) The third strike uses the non-blocking hand and attacks upwards, striking the underside of *uke*'s jaw (roughly half of *tori*'s palm would be under *uke*'s jaw). The motion of the strike, while upwards, again curves. This means that in the event that the palm heel misses the target, the elbow following does not.

9. Upward Rising Block with Knife Hand

This technique is mostly an exercise in understanding target areas and how best to expose them. *Tori* initially blocks a right punch using a left upward rising block (*see* Chapter 3) and takes hold of *uke*'s right arm. *Tori* then draws *uke*'s right arm to the side and down in an anticlockwise motion while at the same time drawing his right elbow upwards and back. *Tori*'s right hand should be formed into a knife hand (*see* Chapter 2), fingers level with his right ear and palm facing outwards. Once *tori* has moved *uke*'s right arm as described the left side of *uke*'s neck should be open and exposed: this is the target area. *Tori* then brings his knife hand in to strike the side of *uke*'s neck using the twisting motion described in Chapter 2 (forehand-style knife hand). There are several things to target on this part of the neck: nerve (brachial plexus origin); blood flow (arterial and venous); muscular disruption and of course the spine itself. Which one you are aiming for will depend on many factors: what outcome you are intending (this range from discomfort right up to death, so be aware of the consequences!), *uke*'s position relative to you (which areas are most accessible) and your own accuracy.

10. Defences against a Double Wrist Grab

Here we have shown three basic escapes but as you progress through any martial art you will learn that there is never any restriction on what can or should be used. You will find yourself in positions that fall outside the category of 'regular' training (because training cannot, and should not, emulate everything that can happen in combat), and in such circumstances you need to allow your body to do the thinking. Your body will know from its position what will work best and what will not. Never restrict yourself to thinking 'I am in position X, I must use technique Y'. Situations are infinitely varied in real combat and the good martial artist (the one who wins) is the one who can adapt and improvise. The martial arts provide the tools for defence; allow the body to select the one that will be most effective.

Upward rising block with knife hand (opening the target).

Upward rising block with knife hand (strike).

Defence against double wrist grab ((i) kick).

Defence against double wrist grab ((i) wrist take).

Defence against double wrist grab ((i) lock).

(i) The initial move in this technique should feel familiar by now, it is the weakener. Here we use a backwards kick, pivoting at the waist and thrusting back with the foot. The target for the kick will depend on what is presented but the groin or a knee will often do the trick. From here *tori* places the kicking foot on the floor near to *uke* and brings the other foot up to join it. At the same time *tori* uses this motion to draw both of his hands upwards, just above his head, palms outwards: this should cause *uke*'s hands to be on the inside of *tori*'s with the thumbs downward. *Tori* now takes hold of *uke*'s left hand with his right, fingers into *uke*'s palm (from the top), with the heel of the palm covering the back of *uke*'s hand and the thumb in the gap between *uke*'s thumb and first finger. *Tori* then applies the lock by turning clockwise underneath *uke*'s raised left arm, pointing *uke*'s fingers to the ground and turning his hand (and body) towards *uke*. Students of *aikido* should recognize sankyo (aikido's third immobilization).

(ii) For this escape begin as for (i) above with the back kick, step in and drawing the arms up. This time however *tori* takes hold of *uke*'s right wrist in his left hand and draws it forward over his shoulder. This should allow *tori* to release his right wrist and bring it back to *uke*'s right shoulder. From here *tori* is in a good position to perform a full shoulder throw (*see* Chapter 10).

(iii) For this escape *tori* begins with a right back kick but this time steps backwards and to the right with the kicking foot, so that the foot ends up just outside *uke*'s right foot, guiding *uke*'s hands around the sides instead of above. Then *tori* brings his left foot back and places it just behind *uke*, fairly centrally. Both knees should be bent so that *tori* is below *uke*'s centre of gravity, and *tori*'s upper body should be bent slightly forward. Keeping his left arm in front of and in contact with *uke*, at about level with *uke*'s abdomen, *tori* twists his upper body anticlockwise. This should have the feeling of sweeping his left arm backwards through *uke*. As *uke* starts to roll backwards over *tori*, *tori* needs to fall backwards with him, bringing his left elbow down on *uke* as they hit the floor (thus using the downward motion in order to add to the effectiveness of the strike).

11. Attacking the Back of the Legs

This set of techniques is as broad as it sounds. Any attack or target *that works* is right! To start people off I have put down a few basic ones here:

(i) Side snap kick to the back of the knee.
(ii) Side snap kick to the back of the calf.
(iii) Roundhouse kick to the inside of the calf.
(iv) Knee strike to the coccyx (base of the spine).
(v) Outwards roundhouse to the inside of the thigh with shin.
(vi) Sliding the instep down the shin.
(vii) Roundhouse to the outside of the lower leg (including the knee).
(viii) Roundhouse to the outside of the upper leg.
(ix) Shin strike to the coccyx/groin.
(x) Straight leg shin strike to the upper leg.

12. Knife Hand to Neck, Kick to Solar Plexus

This is merely an extension of the earlier knife hand technique (technique nine in

Defence against double wrist grab ((ii) drawing arms up).

Defence against double wrist grab ((ii) throw position).

Defence against double wrist grab ((iii) step and strike).

Attacking the backs of the legs ((i) back of the knee).

Attacking the backs of the legs ((ii) back of the calf).

Attacking the backs of the legs ((iii) inside of the calf).

Attacking the backs of the legs ((iv) knee to the coccyx).

Attacking the backs of the legs ((v) inside thigh with shin).

Attacking the backs of the legs ((vi) slide down shin).

Attacking the backs of the legs ((vii) roundhouse to outside of the knee).

Attacking the backs of the legs ((viii) roundhouse to the thigh).

Attacking the backs of the legs ((ix) shin to the coccyx).

Attacking the backs of the legs ((x) straight shin to the upper leg).

this chapter). It is performed as for the knife hand but places a second opponent approaching and requires that *tori* perform a kick to the second opponent (here we are quoting the solar plexus as the target but as mentioned you should use the best target available at the time).

13. Roundhouse Kicks from the Ground

As with all techniques shown from the ground this should not be seen as a position to be in intentionally. These kicks are

Knife hand to neck, kick to solar plexus.

Roundhouse kicks from the ground (knee).

Roundhouse kicks from the ground (groin).

Roundhouse kicks from the ground (solar plexus).

Roundhouse kicks from the ground (solar plexus using the heel).

because you are on the floor and have to work from that position. The kicks are, in essence, identical to the roundhouse kicks described in Chapter 4. The only difference is that the rotation is obtained from rolling the body towards *uke*, rather than pivoting on the non-kicking foot. Here we have shown a few of the main target areas: knee, groin, solar plexus and solar plexus using the heel. While the kicks are effective it is still a better idea not to end up in this position.

14. Combination Kicks

Combination kicks are exactly what they say; they are two or more kicks combined. This could be to take on more than one opponent, to kick an opponent for a second time (if you are having difficulty persuading them to fall over!) or to circumvent their defence. The last reason is the most common; this could mean that *uke* has blocked the first kick and *tori* puts in a secondary kick while *uke*

Combination kicks ((i) low roundhouse).

Combination kicks ((i) high roundhouse).

Combination kicks ((ii) front kick).

Combination kicks ((ii) side thrust kick).

is still concerned with the first block, or *tori* could use the first kick in the combination as a feint to make *uke* commit himself to a defence. I have only described a few here, the description of the individual kicks is covered in Chapter 4 and this is a good area for individual experimentation.

(i) The first is a low roundhouse converted into a high roundhouse to bypass a block.
(ii) The second is a front kick into a side thrust kick.
(iii) The third is a roundhouse kick into a spinning back kick to increase range (where an opponent has moved back to avoid the first kick).

Combination kicks ((iii) roundhouse).

Combination kicks ((iii) spinning back kick).

One-handed throws, right ((i) block and kick).

One-handed throws, right ((i) arm take).

15. One-Handed Throws (right hand)

The reasons for these techniques should be easily discerned (if one hand for some reason or other cannot be used – everything from an injury to carrying a child). As the only usable arm is the right it is best to adjust your stance so that this arm is the one presented to the opponent (so for these techniques use a right foot forward stance).

(i) For this first technique *tori* uses a right cross block (to a right punch). *Tori* takes

One-handed throws, right ((i) lock).

One-handed throws, right ((ii) block).

One-handed throws, right ((ii) arm wrap).

One-handed throws, right ((iii) backfist to ribs).

One-handed throws, right ((iii) full shoulder position).

hold of *uke*'s right hand, thumb on the back with fingers reaching over the top into *uke*'s palm, then uses a right side snap kick to the side of *uke*'s knee. This should cause *uke* to fall to his knee at which time *tori* rotates *uke*'s hand clockwise and turns his body clockwise, thus bringing *uke*'s arm straight and into an armlock. Owing to the restrictions of working one-handed the best finish from here would be for *tori* to bring his knee up sharply into *uke*'s straightened elbow. If you come up with other effective finishes please let me know, I'm always on the lookout for new ideas.

(ii) Defending against a right punch *tori* steps forward with his right foot and uses a right outside forearm parry. In this instance *tori* keeps his right arm rotating clockwise, winding around *uke*'s right arm and trapping it against his own body. *Tori* then pivots on his right foot, bringing his left foot around anticlockwise. As he is performing this motion *tori* needs to be bending his left knee and straightening his right leg out (toes pointing forwards), forming his legs into the body drop position (*see* Chapter 6). When the left foot stops rotating the upper body continues in the same direction drawing *uke* over *tori*'s right leg.

(iii) *Tori* uses a right cross block to *uke*'s right punch then strikes *uke*'s floating ribs

135

One-handed throws, right ((iv) strike to neck).

One-handed throws, right ((iv) rice bail position).

One-handed throws, left ((i) block).

One-handed throws, left ((i) strike to leg).

with a right backfist strike. *Tori* then places *uke*'s arm over his shoulder, taking hold high up on the arm, and performs a full shoulder throw (*see* Chapter 10).

(iv) *Tori* again uses a right cross block and then strikes *uke*'s neck (slightly to the rear) with a knife hand. *Tori* then rolls his arm around the back of *uke*'s neck so that *uke*'s head ends up in the crook of his arm with *tori*'s forearm across his throat. *Tori* then performs a rice bail throw (*see* Chapter 7).

16. One-Handed Throws (left hand)

When defending with the left hand it is

best to be in a normal left short fighting stance.

(i) *Tori* uses a left inside forearm parry and then uses a knife hand to strike at the front of the hip joint of *uke*'s leading leg or to just above the knee. This strike needs to be aiming diagonally downwards and through *uke*'s leg. If done correctly it should have the effect of pinning the leg in place (stopping *uke* from drawing it back) and thus forcing *uke* to the floor (with the continued forward motion from *tori*).

(ii) *Tori* uses a left inside forearm parry, takes hold of *uke*'s upper arm then pivots

One-handed throws, left ((ii) block).

One-handed throws, left ((ii) throw position).

One-handed throws, left ((iii) initial bend of arm).

One-handed throws, left ((iii) lock).

in, placing *uke*'s arm over his right shoulder. *Tori* then performs a full shoulder throw (*see* Chapter 10).

(iii) From an inside forearm parry *tori* continues rotating his left arm anticlockwise while moving in towards *uke*. On the downward arc of the rotation *tori* needs to bring his arm quite low, to cause *uke*'s arm to bend. Once *uke*'s arm is bending *tori* finishes the rotation by bringing his hand up and taking hold of *uke*'s lapel. If *uke*'s arm has bent on the downward part of

the rotation then it will finish up both bent and horizontal (elbow pointing to *tori*'s right), which is a less than comfortable position to be in. To make this even more uncomfortable *tori* needs only to straighten his left arm.

(iv) From a left inside forearm parry *tori* strikes the left side of *uke*'s neck with his left hand then hooks that arm around *uke*'s neck. Pushing his hips through to the left *tori* then performs a neck winding throw (*see* Chapter 10).

One-handed throws, left ((iv) block).

One-handed throws, left ((iv) throw position).

Basic knife defences ((i) strike to elbow).

Basic knife defences ((i) wrist take).

Basic knife defences ((i) finish).

17. Basic Knife Defences

As I have said in the past, and will carry on saying, the best defence against a knife attack is to run like hell! Knife defences are used when you have no option but to stand and fight.

(i) For the first technique (against a right-handed attack) *tori* steps forward and to the left with his left foot and performs a right outside forearm parry. Taking hold of *uke*'s right wrist with his right hand *tori* rotates *uke*'s wrist so that his palm is facing upwards (this means that the back of *tori*'s hand will be turning towards himself); this has the effect of straightening out *uke*'s arm with the elbow underneath. *Tori* then steps forward with his left foot, placing it on the floor directly underneath *uke*'s right elbow, and at the same time brings his left arm sharply up against the underside of *uke*'s extended elbow. Bending his left arm *tori* brings his left hand up to take hold of the other side of *uke*'s wrist (again thumbs on the back and fingers on the palm, which should be facing up). *Tori* then lifts *uke*'s arm, slides his left foot further in front of *uke* then pivots on the left foot for 180 degrees in a clockwise motion. This is done quickly with *tori* keeping a tight hold on *uke*'s hand. *Tori* should end up facing the place that *uke* was standing. I say 'was standing' because if done at full speed with no slipping at the wrist *uke* has a choice of flying through the air or sustaining a severely dislocated wrist (to add to the broken arm he received earlier in the technique). The picture shows *uke* still standing to let you *see* your finish position relative to where *uke* was. In training you will need to allow your hands to slip slightly or you'll soon be looking for a new partner.

(ii) Defending against a straight thrust *tori* steps forward and to the left with his left foot. At the same time *tori* brings his right arm up on the inside of *uke*'s wrist and his left arm up against the outside of *uke*'s elbow. In the same motion *tori* slams his left arm forward into the elbow while drawing his right arm back sharply. It doesn't take much imagination to guess the result!

(iii) Defending against a straight thrust *tori* steps forward and to the left with his left foot and performs a right outside forearm parry. While still moving *tori* draws his left hand back as if to strike *uke*'s neck with a knife hand. Rather than striking the neck

Basic knife defences ((ii) straight arm-break).

Basic knife defences ((iii) forearm strike to neck).

Basic knife defences ((iii) neck wrap).

Basic knife defences ((iv) parry and collect).

Basic knife defences ((iv) return to sender).

with the knife hand *tori* strikes the front of *uke*'s neck with his forearm. If this can be done as part of the parry while *uke* is still moving into the strike, so much the better. *Tori* continues the anticlockwise rotation of his left arm in order to wrap his arm around *uke*'s neck, bending him backwards. While this is going on *tori* pulls *uke*'s right arm tight across his chest. This has the double effect of an armlock and a neck lock.

(iv) From a downward 'ice pick' style attack *tori* again steps forwards and to the left with his left foot. At the same time he brings his right hand up as if to do a right outside forearm parry. This time however, instead of directing the blow further away to *tori*'s right, *tori* directs the blow down-

wards (in the direction it is already going). By pushing the attacking hand further around its arc than *uke* intended *tori* can bring it back up into *uke*'s body.

18. Reverse Body Drop

This throw 'does exactly what it says on the box'. *Tori*'s body motions are the same as for a body drop but *uke* is being thrown backwards. *Tori* uses a left inside forearm parry (from a right punch attack), moving into the block in the same way as for the outer reaping throw (*see* Chapter 7) by placing his left foot level with and on the outside of *uke*'s right foot. *Tori* brings his right foot up next to his left and then extends it behind *uke* (left knee bent, right

Reverse body drop.

Reverse dropping body drop (initial position).

Reverse dropping body drop (throw).

leg straight, toes of right foot facing forwards). At the same time *tori* brings his right arm up to strike the front of *uke*'s neck bringing *uke* over *tori*'s extended right leg.

19. Reverse Dropping Body Drop

Again we draw a parallel, this time with the regular dropping body drop (*see* Chapter 9). As with the previous technique *tori* steps forward into an inside forearm parry and brings both feet up together outside *uke*'s right foot. This time *tori*'s right hand should already be in place at *uke*'s neck. Sliding his right leg out straight behind *uke*'s legs *tori* lowers himself onto his left knee. Drawing his right arm forwards and his left arm across his front finishes the throw.

12 *Shodan*

1. Throw Sequence

This is part of the *shodan* (first-degree black belt) grading, the first of the *dan* grades, but it does not bring in anything new. It is as it says a sequence of throws, normally done using four or so *uke* who attack one after the other until the examiner is satisfied that *tori* has demonstrated the basic throws to a sufficiently high standard (usually between twenty-five and thirty). It is designed, at the very beginning of the grading, to put *tori* under pressure both physically and mentally. As well as examining his knowledge of the fundamental throws it also tests his endurance and spirit. Each *dan* grading is individual to the candidate and the examiner will deliberately take the student to what the student believes is his limit, and then past it to the real limit. I have included a sequence here but if you are taking your *shodan* it is up to you.

(i) Hip throw.
(ii) Sweeping loin.
(iii) Spring hip.
(iv) Hip wheel.
(v) Neck wheel.
(vi) Transitional hip throw.
(vii) Leg wheel.
(viii) One-arm shoulder throw.
(ix) Body drop shoulder throw.
(x) Full shoulder.
(xi) Reverse full shoulder.
(xii) Inner wind.
(xiii) Outer wind.
(xiv) Body drop.
(xv) Reverse body drop.
(xvi) Dropping body drop.
(xvii) Reverse dropping body drop.
(xviii) Cross ankle throw.
(xix) Outer reaping throw.
(xx) Inner reaping throw.
(xxi) Outer hook.
(xxii) Outer wheel.
(xxiii) Front scoop.
(xxiv) Back scoop.
(xxv) Shoulder wheel.

2. Counter-Techniques

This section of techniques focuses on preventing an opponent using a technique on us and using his position to allow us to use our technique on them.

(i) Here *uke* is attacking with a hip throw (*see* Chapter 5). *Tori* drops his weight down below *uke*'s centre of gravity by bending his knees (bearing in mind that *uke*'s objective is to get his hips below *tori*'s centre of gravity) while at the same time striking *uke*'s kidney with his left palm heel. With his right arm around the front of *uke*'s waist *tori* then leans backwards, to bring *uke* off balance, and twists to the left to bring *uke* backwards over him.

(ii) Here *uke* is coming in for a body drop (*see* Chapter 6). As *uke* is putting his right leg in place *tori* steps over with his right foot and places it directly in front of *uke*, in between *uke*'s legs. *Tori* allows his body to

Counter-techniques ((i) initial blocking of throw).

Counter-techniques ((i) counter-throw).

Counter-techniques ((ii) step over body drop).

Counter-techniques ((ii) counter-hook).

continue rotating in the same direction (anticlockwise) pivoting on his right foot. As part of this motion *tori* brings his left leg up behind *uke*'s right leg and, as part of the rotation, hooks *uke*'s leg up, back and to *tori*'s left. As this is being done *tori* pushes *uke* backwards with his right forearm across *uke*'s throat.

(iii) Here *uke* is coming in for a one-arm shoulder throw. *Tori* bends his right arm downward and steps just in front of *uke*'s right foot with his right foot. *Tori* then pivots on his right foot to turn in front of *uke*, at the same time hooking his right arm under *uke*'s right arm. *Tori* is now in a position to perform a body drop shoulder throw (*see* Chapter 8).

(iv) In this counter *tori* uses an outer reaping throw against an outer reaping throw (*see* Chapter 7). The most important part of this counter is to block the strike aimed by *uke* at *tori*'s neck. While doing this *tori* rotates his right arm clockwise to bring it inside *uke*'s original blocking arm. *Uke* will already be moving forward in order to do the outer reaping throw so *tori* only needs to move his left foot a small distance to bring it alongside *uke*'s right foot. *Tori* then

Counter-techniques ((iii) arm turn).

Counter-techniques ((iii) pivot).

Counter-techniques ((iii) throw).

Counter-techniques ((iv) counter-block).

Counter-techniques ((iv) throw).

completes the outer reaping throw as already described.

3. Inner Thigh Throw

There are two main ways of doing an inner thigh throw, although these are just the ends of a spectrum. You could fill a book with the variations that lie between these two but, if you are training correctly, your body will naturally move into these variations (indeed unless you and your *uke* are exactly the same build, size, temperament, have the same training and end up in the same positions as the people in the photos I would hope it is a slight variation that you are doing).

(i) This first inner thigh throw starts with *tori* blocking a right punch with a left inside forearm parry. *Tori* then takes hold of *uke*'s right arm with his left and places his right foot in between *uke*'s feet. *Tori* then brings his left foot up next to his right so that he is at a right angle to *uke*, at the same time placing his right arm around *uke*'s waist. As he is coming in *tori* needs to bend his knees, straightening them when they are underneath *uke*'s centre of gravity. This has the effect of lifting *uke* onto his toes (as with the spring hip in Chapter 9). In a continuation of this motion *tori* sweeps his right leg backwards directly between *uke*'s legs while pulling forwards and around with his arms.

(ii) In this variation *tori* blocks the right punch with a right outside forearm parry. Taking hold of *uke*'s right forearm with his right hand *tori* pivots on his right foot and brings his left hand sharply into *uke*'s elbow. From here *tori* sweeps his left leg in front of *uke* then sharply back to sweep *uke*'s right leg at roughly knee level. *Tori*'s left arm (into the elbow) and left leg should be going forwards at the same time thus causing *uke* to be off balance (heading forwards) as *tori*'s left leg sweeps into his leg (try this left-handed then look at the first variation and you will *see* what I mean by the moves being two ends of a spectrum).

4. Combinations

Combinations are what combat is all about. By reaching this stage you should already be using combinations as part of your normal training as it is very rare in real combat to be 100 per cent successful

Inner thigh ((i) initial position).

Inner thigh ((i) throw).

Inner thigh ((ii) throw position).

Combination throws ((i) hip throw blocked).

Combination throws ((i) turning into inner reaping).

with your first technique and to not need any more. In essence a combination is where an initial technique has not worked and *tori* moves from that technique to another that is more appropriate. The technique not working could be due to *uke* blocking or a misjudgement by *tori* (which usually comes when *tori* uses his mind to decide what technique to use ahead of time, instead of using his body to decide what will work best).

(i) Here *tori* is coming in for a hip throw and *uke* is stopping the technique by leaning backwards. By its very nature this defence (on its own), while stopping the forward throw, puts *uke* off balance backwards. This is not apparent while *tori* is trying to throw forwards as the two forces are balanced. This means that the best way to throw *uke* at this point is backwards; if *tori* changes direction quickly enough *uke* is pulling themselves in the direction of the throw, helping *tori*. Here *tori* changes direction and brings his right forearm up to the right side of *uke*'s neck. As they are turning *tori* hooks his right leg behind *uke*'s left leg. *Tori* then completes an inner reaping throw (*see* Chapter 7).

(ii) Here *uke* is blocking *tori*'s outer reaping attack by using the block mentioned previously in section two (iv) of this chapter. Because he is expecting to resist a throw taking him backwards his balance is shifted forwards. *Tori* uses this balance in order to throw *uke* forwards using a rear throw (*see* Chapter 10). *Tori* leaves his feet in the forward position alongside *uke*'s right foot and brings his right hand down to strike *uke*'s stomach. Keeping hold of *uke*'s right arm with his left, and keeping his right hand in *uke*'s stomach, *tori* allows his body to fall directly across *uke*'s legs. As *uke* starts to fall forward *tori* projects him further using his right hand.

Combination throws ((ii) outer reaping blocked).

Combination throws ((ii) into rear throw).

Combination throws ((iii) one-armed shoulder throw blocked).

Combination throws ((iii) arm into position).

(iii) Here *tori* attacks with a one-arm shoulder throw and *uke* blocks it. On this occasion *uke* has blocked by dropping his weight so there is no balance advantage to be gained here. *Tori* keeps *uke*'s right wrist high (with his left hand) but brings his right hand down on the inside of *uke*'s right elbow causing it to bend. *Tori* then turns clockwise bringing *uke*'s right wrist backwards. From here *tori* takes hold of *uke*'s right wrist with his own right wrist. Note that *tori*'s right forearm remains behind *uke*'s arm and that *tori* has made sure that *uke*'s wrist has been moved back sufficiently so that *uke* is off balance when the lock is applied (otherwise this becomes a battle of strength).

(iv) *Tori* attacks with an inner reaping throw to *uke*'s left leg. *Uke* counters by lifting the leg and moving it backwards out of *tori*'s reach. This motion means that for a short period of time all of *uke*'s weight is on his right leg and it is difficult for him to move this leg quickly. *Tori* uses this fact and changes the direction of his push from back and right to back and left. *Tori* at the same time swings the attacking right leg back across to sweep the inside back of *uke*'s right leg.

Combination throws ((iv) into inner reaping).

Combination throws ((iv) uke steps out).

Combination throws ((iv) inner hook).

I always get asked the 'what if' question when teaching these (and other) techniques. 'What if' *uke* counters your combination or your counter (and so on)? The answer is that this is the nature of combat; the two opponents will counter each other's attacks and use multiple combinations until one makes a mistake. There is no such thing as a foolproof technique that always works and does not need a back up. Any *sensei* that tells you a technique is foolproof or unstoppable should be taken with a pinch of salt! The only real advice is to not stop fighting until you've won.

5. Combination Strikes

This is an exercise in using combination punches, different punches and different targets. In the example shown *tori* starts with a left lunge punch (stepping forward with the leading leg being on the same side as the hand that is punching) to the sternum. Keeping the legs in place but rotating the hips into each *tori* then follows up with a right punch to the chin then a left punch to the solar plexus.

There are several reasons for this exercise. It is practise in using several different types of punches: left lunge punch, right cross and left jab (*see* Chapter 2). It also practises targeting different areas of the body: sternum, chin and solar plexus. Finally it practises using the most appropriate strike for a given area, a lunge punch (very powerful) to the sternum (hard target), a left cross (medium power, medium speed) to the jaw (a semi-hard target) and a right jab (low power, high speed) to the solar plexus (soft target).

It is important to remember that the power and hardness quoted here are relative to each other, an individuals lunge punch can produce far more power than a jab, but a jab can shatter a sternum (this takes training!). The point here is to use the most effective weapon at your disposal for the circumstances.

6. Unarmed *Kata*

For this section of the *shodan* the student needs to develop their own *kata* (sequence of training exercises) of blocks, comprising many (or all) of the blocks and parries they have learned, putting in appropriate counterstrikes and having a *kata* that flows. Most students use a *kata* developed by their *sensei* (or even their *sensei*'s *sensei*) which is fine provided the student understands what they are doing and is not repeating the *kata* by rote. The whole point of a *kata* is to enable the student to train solo, conditioning their body to flow into blocks and strikes without the need to think about it. Remember this if you remember nothing else; a *kata* can be an aid to training as a means to an end, it is not an end unto itself! An example *kata* is shown in Chapter 18.

7. Cross Block, Backfist to Ear with Throw

This is another technique that requires the students to do some thinking for themselves. All that is required is for *tori* to use a right cross block (*see* Chapter 3), take hold of *uke*'s right arm with his left hand and strike *uke*'s right ear with a right backfist (*see* Chapter 2). From here *tori* needs to demonstrate any technique that they feel works best from this position (at least three: if they don't appear to the examiner to work properly *tori* may find themselves doing more). In terms of combat this is to encourage the use of a block that isn't frequently used and to combine it with appropriate techniques. The reason being that while everyone has favourite blocks,

Combination strikes (lunge punch to sternum).

Combination strikes (right cross to chin).

Combination strikes (left jab to solar plexus).

Cross block with backfist to ear (cross block).

Cross block with backfist to ear (backfist to ear).

strikes and techniques (which is human nature) they may not always be the most appropriate response to the situation you are in. A good example exists in simple DIY: while it is possible to take off a nut using a pair of pliers it is easier and more effective to use a spanner (but bear in mind that sometimes you may be forced to use the pliers: think about it).

One of my favourites from this position is the outer winding throw (*see* Chapter 10). Try it and others to *see* what works for you.

8. Counters to Kicks

An important factor in defence against any kicks is to move yourself out of the way! Leg muscles are stronger than arm muscles so it is best not to rely too much on the block without any avoidance. Defence against kicks should be taught from an early stage, here we test how well the student can adapt them to fluid (combat) situations.

(i) Front Kick

The defence I have shown here is the easiest to perform, and one of the most effective. Defending against a right front

snap kick *tori* moves his left foot forwards and outwards at a forty-five degree angle and then swings his left arm across to the right to strike *uke*'s lower leg (using a ridge hand, *see* Chapter 2). As he is striking *tori* brings his right leg across to the left, thus moving his body out of the path of the kick. This strike throws *uke* off to the right (using his own redirected forward momentum) and leaves his back open to attack by *tori*. Because *tori*'s body is moving fully out of *uke*'s way this would work just as well as a defence against the crescent kick.

(ii) Side Thrust Kick

Because of the power of this kick it is doubly important for *tori* to get his body out of the path of the kick. Here we see *tori* stepping forward and to the right with his right leg while at the same time bringing his left leg across to the right. As the legs are moving *tori* brings his right arm across to the left, as if he was doing a cross block on *uke*'s knee, and hooks his left arm behind *uke*'s leg and pulls it towards him. This scissoring action on *uke*'s leg can have a profound effect on him so be careful in practise. As the force of this kick is directed at a right angle to the cross block

Counters to kicks ((i) ridge hand block).

Counters to kicks ((i) finish off).

Counters to kicks ((ii) strike to knee from side thrust kick).

Counters to kicks ((iii) inside parry from crescent kick).

tori does not have to block any of the force of the kick (as a variation try using a palm heel strike with the right hand instead of a cross block).

(iii) Crescent

As mentioned (i) works well against this. Another defence (shown here) starts with *tori* stepping forward and to the right with his right foot and bringing his left foot across to the right. As he is doing this *tori* hooks his left arm under *uke*'s attacking leg. *Tori* keeps his left leg moving in a semicircular path (anticlockwise) until he

Counters to kicks ((iii) sweep).

Counters to kicks ((iv) step into spinning back kick).

Counters to kicks ((iv) sweep).

Counters to kicks ((v) roundhouse take).

Counters to kicks ((v) throw).

is facing the same direction as *uke*; at which point *tori* stops his left foot and sweeps *uke*'s non-kicking leg with his right.

(iv) Spinning Back Kick

This defence requires a great deal of confidence in order to pull it off correctly because it involves going against your instincts. As *uke* starts to spin (anticlockwise here to kick with his left foot) *tori* moves straight in at him bringing him right up to *uke*'s back. *Tori* hooks his left arm under the kicking leg (which due to his position has passed by his left side) and sweeps *uke*'s right leg with his right leg.

(v) Roundhouse Kick

A simple defence to this is very similar to the defence against the side thrust kick above. The arm and leg movements are identical but instead of the left leg just moving across it keeps moving in an anti-clockwise semicircle. This has two main results: the first is that by rotating in sync with the rotation of the kick you absorb the majority of its power without ill effect, the second is that *uke* is expecting his motion to be stopped and is thus unprepared for the continuing rotation which will cause him to fall.

Counters to kicks ((vi) side snap kick avoidance).

Counters to kicks ((vi) counter snap kick).

One-handed throat throw (initial take).

One-handed throat throw (throw).

(vi) Side Snap

The main defence for these kicks are simple to describe and difficult to achieve. As mentioned this quick kick would normally be aimed at the opponent's lead knee. To defend *tori* draws his lead leg up and out of the way of the attack then, as *uke* starts to put his foot down, allows his raised leg to follow *uke*'s back down. As *uke*'s foot touches the floor *tori* continues following the motion with his lead leg and performs a side snap kick on *uke*'s lead knee. Put simply if *uke* tries to do a side snap kick, you draw your leg up out of the way and do it back to him.

9. One-Handed Throat Throw

This technique is as simple as it is dangerous. Using an inside forearm block from a right punch *tori* moves in close in the same way as for the outer reaping move (*see* Chapter 7). As he is moving in *tori* strikes at *uke*'s throat with his right hand, using the 'v' between the thumb and first finger (thumb to the left of the throat and fingers to the right). The strike is aimed for just below the Adam's apple on a man (halfway up on a woman) and is directed back and up. Once *uke* is in motion from the strike *tori* redirects his striking hand downwards

153

(still backwards) putting *uke* onto the floor. In training please bear in mind how dangerous this can be, mistakes happen to the best of us. I remember having a very sore neck from this technique, at Prescot Leisure Centre from a training partner of mine. That particular partner is one of the best *ju-jitsuka* I've ever trained with, so if it can happen to him it could happen to you (remember that one, Mr Daintry?).

10. Attacking the Ears and Eyes

(a) The Ears
Here we are examining the various ways to attack the ears, something that can cause anything from mild stunning through to permanent damage. Most are self-explanatory, utilizing strikes we have already covered (*see* Chapter 2), aimed at the ears, and so I won't go into detail with them.

- Knife hand, forehand.
- Ridge hand.
- Flat-handed slap.
- Bottom fist (hammer fist).
- Cupped hand slap.
- Backfist.
- Knife hand, backhanded.

This list is only a guide and there are plenty more, your imagination is your only

Attacking the ears (forehand knife hand).

Attacking the ears (ridge hand).

Attacking the ears (flat-handed slap).

Attacking the ears (bottom fist).

Attacking the ears (cupped hand slap).

Attacking the ears (backfist).

Attacking the ears (backhanded knife hand).

Attacking the eyes (two fingers straight).

restriction. Just bear in mind practicality though: a knee to the ear is very effective if they are bent double but not if they are standing straight!

(b) The Eyes

As with attacking the ears the strikes are mostly self explanatory but again bear in mind the outcome of using these techniques: from a watering eye to permanent blindness!

- Two fingers straight.
- Two fingers clawed (this involves a flick of the wrist).

Attacking the eyes (two fingers clawed).

155

Attacking the eyes (fingers flicked).

Attacking the eyes (finger reinforced).

Attacking the eyes (thumb).

Attacking the eyes (first knuckle).

Attacking the eyes (second knuckle).

Attacking the eyes (strike to nose).

X block defences (block).

- Fingers flicked (fingers spread and flicked horizontally across the eyes).
- Finger reinforced (first and second fingers extended tight together).
- Thumb extended from fist.
- First knuckle extended from fist.
- Second knuckle extended from fist.
- Strike to point of nose (this is here because it has the effect of making the eyes water).

11. X Block Defences

Here is a practical practise of the X block (*see* Chapter 3). *Tori* meets a downward strike with an X block, right hand on top. *Tori* then twists his hands towards himself to trap *uke*'s attacking arm. *Tori* then pulls *uke* forward, at the same time bringing in a knee strike to whatever target presents itself: here the floating ribs.

X block defences (drawing onto knee).

Left and right upward block (first block).

Left and right upward block (second block).

12. Left and Right Upward Block with Throw

As with the cross block with a backfist to the ear earlier *tori* needs to find his own techniques from this start and as before they need to be effective, not showy. This double block also reminds the student that his opponent has more than just a right hand; a right punch is not going to be the end of the attack.

Uke starts with a right punch to the face and will then follow up with a left to the face. *Tori* uses a left upwards rising block against the first strike pulling *uke* off balance (to the left and downwards). This reduces the effectiveness and accuracy of *uke*'s second strike, which will tend to come overhead because of the movement. *Tori* uses a right upward rising block against this second punch. From this position *tori* needs to complete with whatever seems most effective.

One of my preferences (but only one, I'm not going to make it that easy for you) is the neck winding throw (*see* Chapter 10).

13. Sparring Defence against Kicks

For the grading this is exactly as it says. *Uke* will attack with random kicks and *tori* needs to defend against them. The difference here from the earlier practice is that the kicks are random, in a moving environment, and will not stop until *tori* effectively counters *uke*. That is to say that *tori* needs to counter the kicks, not just block them: if he doesn't *uke* will keep kicking. Once the first *uke* has been countered a second will start. It is normal to use four *uke* who rotate until the examiner is satisfied, both with technique and spirit.

14. All Palm Heel Blocks

Tori needs to be able to demonstrate palm heel blocks from random punches and kicks. Here it is only necessary to demonstrate a block and strike (that are effective).

15. Use of all Body Weapons

This is normally done as a demonstration

against an unmoving target (a three-dimensional target). It is used for the student to demonstrate their knowledge of not only the use of all body weapons (all punches, knife hands, ridge hands, spear hands, bottom fist, elbows and so on, *see* Chapter 2) but also their knowledge of *atemi* (strike) points on the body *and* the most effective combination of strike and *atemi* points. This shows the student's knowledge of the different effects of the various strikes, for example, due to its small striking area the force applied to a spear hand produces very high pressure but it is most effective on the 'soft' targets where high penetration is desirable, such as the lymph glands (armpit) or throat.

16. Most Effective Throw or Technique

Here the student must choose, demonstrate and justify their own four most effective techniques. This is a reminder that everyone has favourites, and it is usually because those techniques are the most effective for that individual. It is also a reminder that because of the effectiveness of those techniques the body is more likely to use them when in a stress position. After the *shodan* the student will work at removing the thought of individual techniques and replacing it with the feeling that the body itself is the weapon and it has an infinite spectrum of movements that it can call upon. Basically the student will learn to trust their own body (although there is a great deal of hard work ahead for the body to earn that trust).

17. Most Effective Strikes

As for the techniques so for the strikes, need I say more?

18. Teaching Practice

This is something I require of all students before they take their *shodan*. I want to *see* that they can pass on the knowledge, without bias to their own preferences. Teaching is a skill that can be learned only through experience. Some have the gift and some do not, what I look for is *improvement* in a person's teaching ability.

19. Everything Else You've Ever Done!

As a *shodan* you have a responsibility to pass on everything you have learned to your students, wholesale and without bias (they have to choose their path just as you did). This means that after you have finished the other parts of the *shodan* the examiner will ask for demonstrations of as many techniques from any syllabus they like (or all).

If you think you can breathe a sigh of relief after passing your *shodan* you are both right and terribly wrong! For many people this is their only aim, which is not a bad thing if it helps them to strive to better themselves. Unfortunately most of you will find on passing this grade that it only opens you up to how much there is to learn, again not a bad thing. Passing the *shodan* you have completed your apprenticeship, you are now a journeyman with quite a way to go before you can call yourself a master. For me it was when the real challenges (and fun) really began and I hope it is for you.

13 Short Stick Work

1. Figure-Four Armlock

The basic grip on the short stick can be seen here, a couple of inches of the stick showing below the little finger, the rest above the hand. For the figure-four lock *tori* uses the stick to perform a cross block to a right punch (*see* Chapter 3 for full descriptions of the blocks referred to, these are no different they just use a weapon to assist). *Tori* then takes hold of *uke*'s right wrist with his left hand and uses the bottom of the short stick to strike at *uke*'s floating ribs. *Tori* then brings the stick up under *uke*'s extended arm, so that it now points straight up, then brings it back sharply against *uke*'s elbow. This causes *uke*'s arm to bend which *tori* uses to push *uke*'s wrist behind the top of the short stick. *Tori* now takes hold of the top of the stick with his left hand and twists the stick anticlockwise (left hand down, right hand up).

2. Extended Arm Immobilization

Starting from a cross block and strike, as described in section one, *tori* then places the stick over *uke*'s right shoulder (from behind) so that it comes to rest under *uke*'s chin. To do this the thumb of the hand holding the stick should be touching the top of *uke*'s shoulder blade and the stick should rest in the junction between *uke*'s shoulder and neck muscles. To apply the lock *tori* pulls down on the stick (causing *uke*'s neck to extend) and pushes *uke*'s straight right arm straight ahead.

Figure-four armlock (block).

Figure-four armlock (strike to ribs).

Figure-four armlock (strike to side of elbow).

Figure-four armlock (lock).

3. Rice Bail Choke

Here we start again with a cross block but instead of striking to the floating ribs *tori* strikes to the side of the neck with the bottom of the stick. From here *tori* wraps his arm around the neck in the same way as for the rice bail throw described in Chapter 7. Instead of using his wrist to apply pressure to *uke*'s throat however, *tori* uses the stick itself by taking hold of the free end in his left hand. At this point *tori* can either complete the rice bail throw in the same way as for the orange belt syllabus or continue onto the very effective lock shown. To do the secondary lock *tori*, keeping his hands in position, slides his left forearm over the top of *uke*'s head (keeping tight to the head at all times) until both forearms come together. To apply the lock *tori* just pulls both hands towards him while keeping his elbows out (carefully, this is very powerful when done correctly).

Extended arm immobilization.

Rice bail choke (strike to neck).

Rice bail choke (rice bail choke).

Rice bail choke (continuation to side lock).

X crossing wrist lock (block).

4. X Crossing Wrist Lock

Tori uses an outside parry against a right punch, as for the outside forearm parry (right arm) but using the stick as the blocking surface. Shown here the parry is reinforced using the left palm on the upper part of the stick. *Tori* then transfers the stick to the opposite side of *uke*'s arm at the wrist joint, still pointing up, and takes hold of the upper part of the stick in his left hand with the thumb uppermost. From here *tori* lowers his hands and twists clockwise so that his arms cross at the wrist. To apply the wrist lock *tori* pulls

X crossing wrist lock (initial position).

X crossing wrist lock (wrist lock).

X crossing wrist lock (extended armlock).

Back scoop (initial strike).

Back scoop (throw).

back with his hands and pushes forward with his elbows. To turn into the armlock *tori* keeps *uke*'s hand locked (with *tori*'s wrists remaining touching) and moves his left elbow forward and under *uke*'s elbow. At the same time *tori* extends *uke*'s arm so that the back of the elbow is at its maximum extension pivoted over *tori*'s arm.

5. Back Scoop

Here *tori* uses an ordinary left inside forearm parry to a right punch and at the same time allows the short stick to move in his grip so that an equal amount of stick is showing on either side of the hand. *Tori*

then strikes through between *uke*'s legs so that the upper part of the stick (the section above the thumb) strikes the groin on the way through. Once the stick is through *tori* twists it clockwise until it is horizontal then performs a rear scoop throw (as described in Chapter 9), using the stick (rather than needing to grab with the right hand).

6. Entangled Armlock

This lock is identical to the one described in Chapter 8 but uses the stick as the bar to apply the lock giving greater leverage. *Tori* uses a left inside forearm parry to a

Entangled armlock (initial stick position).

Entangled armlock (hand take).

Entangled armlock (lock).

right punch then strikes the floating ribs with the stick. The stick is then placed between *uke*'s body and his left arm, level with his elbow. *Tori* then takes hold of the upper part of the stick (over the top of *uke*'s arm). Keeping the stick on *uke*'s elbow *tori* moves his right forearm onto *uke*'s left forearm pushing it away from him while pulling the upper part of the stick; this has the effect of bending *uke*'s arm. *Tori* then pivots on his right foot, bringing his left foot around in an anticlockwise semicircle. While doing this *tori* continues the anticlockwise twisting of the stick until it is horizontal. Thereafter any raising of *tori*'s right hand will apply the lock.

7. Front Scoop

This is performed in the same way as the front scoop from Chapter 9. The only differences are that it is done from *uke*'s left side and the stick is used for the strikes and pivot. *Tori* uses an inside forearm parry then strikes *uke* to the solar plexus with the short stick while stepping with the right foot so that it is level with *uke*'s left foot. The strike to the solar plexus should cause *uke* to bend but regardless *tori* also strikes to the medulla oblongata (*see* Appendix) with a left knife hand. *Tori* keeps hold of the neck in his left hand and strikes through *uke*'s legs with the short stick. By turning the stick horizontally *tori* then completes the front scoop throw.

8. Crossing Neck Lock with Throw

For this technique *tori* allows the stick to slip so that only a few inches of the upper part (by the thumb) are showing. *Tori* holds the stick along the inside of his forearm and does a cross block to *uke*'s punch.

Front scoop (strike across body).

Front scoop (throw).

Crossing neck lock with throw (initial
stick position).

Crossing neck lock with throw (lock).

Tori then brings the bottom of the stick
behind *uke*'s neck, done in such a way that
tori's wrist strikes the side of *uke*'s neck
sharply. Up until this point it is best for *tori*
to keep hold of *uke*'s right wrist with his
left hand (it can still be used against you).
Tori now reaches with his left hand, over
his right forearm, to grasp the end of the
stick on the far side of *uke*'s neck. This in
itself is a powerful strangle but to finish off
tori uses this grip and turns his body into a
body drop throw (*see* Chapter 6), finishing
off with a short stick strike.

Crossing neck lock with throw (throw).

Rear choke (application).

9. Rear Choke

Tori performs an outside parry (as for section four) and then strikes *uke*'s neck with the butt of stick while stepping behind him. *Tori* then slides the stick around the front of *uke*'s neck and grabs the top of the stick in his left hand, palm down. To apply the neck lock *tori* draws his hands back and pushes his elbows into *uke*'s back.

10. Defences against Front Snap Kick

Shown here we have two defences against a right front snap kick; they both start identically and just the finish differs. For both *tori* steps forward and to the left at a forty-five degree angle with his left leg. At the same time *tori* brings his right arm down as if doing a downward inside forearm parry (*see* Chapter 3). Instead of making the parry with the right arm *tori* uses the stick to strike the side of, and just underneath, *uke*'s calf/shin area. *Tori* then allows the stick to carry on around the bottom of *uke*'s calf until it is vertical on the far side of the leg.

For the first lock the stick is left vertical and *tori* takes hold of the upper part in his left hand so that his thumb is uppermost and his left forearm is resting over the shin. To apply the lock *tori* lets his left elbow drop, so that it is vertical and running along the side of *uke*'s shin, then pulls his hands towards him while pushing the elbows away.

For the second lock *tori* allows the stick to come further round so that it is resting

Defence against front snap kick (lock first position).

Defence against front snap kick (lock second position).

across the top of *uke*'s shin. *Tori* then takes hold of the top of the stick in his left hand with the thumbs facing towards each other. At this stage *uke*'s heel should be resting just over the crook of *tori*'s right elbow. To apply the lock *tori* keeps his body

and elbows where they are and pushes down with both hands.

Be careful with both of these, they are more painful than they look (as one of my instructors found out!).

11. Entangled Armlock (right side)

For the right-side back hammer lock *tori* uses the stick to do an outside forearm parry then points the stick downwards on the inside of *uke*'s elbow. Turning the stick so that it points slightly towards himself *tori* then places the 'V' of his left thumb and forefinger on the underside of the stick. Keeping his right forearm in contact with *uke*'s right forearm *tori* then rotates the stick clockwise (so that the left hand moves away from him and his right hand towards him), which brings them into the entangled armlock position. Continued rotation applies the lock.

Entangled arm lock on the right arm (initial stick position).

Entangled arm lock on the right arm (initial take).

167

14 *Nunchaka* Work

Although the *nunchaka* is an Okinawan weapon and as such belongs to karate there is a very good reason for its study to be here in a ju-jitsu syllabus. Remembering our history several weapons were derived as part of Okinawan karate from farm implements to be used against the samurai, who in turn used ju-jitsu. These included:

- the *nunchaka* (two twelve-inch cylinders of wood connected by a piece of chain or cord);
- the *sai* (long knife with cylindrical or hexagonal blade with two curling prongs as hilt guards); and
- the *tonfa* (wooden baton with a perpendicular handle roughly one-third of the way down).

To defend against a weapon properly it is best to know something about how the weapon is used, hence over the years the study of these Okinawan weapons has been incorporated into many ju-jitsu syllabi (a comparative study if you will).

The first misconception to get out of the way is that the *nunchaka* is used solely for swinging around to look impressive. Not true! The swings, sweeps and passes from hand to hand you will see in this *kata* are designed to improve the student's dexterity with the weapon. They also assist in regaining control of the weapon after it has struck something. Remember that this is a flexible weapon and as such once it has hit something it requires extra skill to bring it

back under control. Have a go on a punch-bag to *see* for yourself.

The second misconception is that it is a striking-only weapon. You will *see* from the *kata* that there are locks and throws as well. I have not included individual techniques in this chapter, as this is only an introduction to the weapon.

Lastly remember that this, like every other weapon, is an extension of your unarmed techniques. If you can do it unarmed then most likely it can be done with the weapon. You need to get to a stage with weapons where you are not consciously using a weapon; you are instead just accepting its various advantages and just doing ju-jitsu.

Start this *kata* with the *nunchaka* in your belt at the back chain ends pointing down.

1. Start with feet together, hands at the side.
2. Step back with the right leg, take hold of the *nunchaka* in the right hand and present your left arm in a defensive position to the front (i).
3. Bring the right foot up level with the left, bring the *nunchaka* to the front, take hold with both hands and extend horizontally (ii).
4. Stepping forward with the right leg, turn the right palm uppermost, bend the right arm to a right angle and bring the left hand down to the outside of the right elbow (iii).

5. Let go with the left hand and swing the *nunchaka* in a figure of eight (iv).
6. After two figures of eight bring the free end to rest under the armpit (v).
7. Flick the *nunchaka* to strike outwards (vi).
8. Recover back to the armpit (vii).
9. Strike downwards again (viii).
10. Bring *nunchaka* over the right shoulder to catch it with the left hand under the right armpit (ix).
11. Bring the left leg up level with the right and present the *nunchaka* out horizontally at arm's length (x).

(i)

(ii)

(iii)

(iv)

(v)

(vi)

(vii)

(viii)

(ix)

(x)

(xi)

(xii)

(xiii)

(xiv)

(xv)

(xvi)

(xvii)

12–18. As for four to ten but on the left side (xi–xvii).

19. From position eighteen release with the left hand and swing the *nunchaka* in a wide arc down and then up over the right shoulder, catching the bottom of the *nunchaka* in the left hand again as shown while stepping back with the left leg (xviii).

20. This time release with the right hand, swing it down then up over the left shoulder, catching with the right while stepping back with the right leg (identical to xvii).

21. Release with the left hand and bring the *nunchaka* down then up over the right shoulder, angled to the left, catching the lower end behind the back in the palm of the left hand. While doing this step back with the left leg (xx).

22. Reverse twenty-one. Release with the right, bring the *nunchaka* over the left shoulder (angled right), catch in the right palm behind the back, and step back with the right foot (xxi).

23. Release with the left hand and swing the *nunchaka* horizontally to the left

(xviii)

(xvix)

(xx)

(xxi)

(xxii)

(xxiii)

stepping forward with the right foot (xxii).

24. Arrest the motion of the *nunchaka* and start to bring it back to the right. The *nunchaka* is brought up diagonally left to right with an anticlockwise semicircle at head height and then brought down diagonally from left to right. Step back with the right leg while doing this (xxiii).

25. Bring the *nunchaka* to rest, hanging down by the right leg (xxiv).

26. Take hold of the lower half with the left hand then bring that section up as if using it to perform an outside parry to a right punch (the right-hand section should be directly underneath) (xxv).

27. Leaving the left-hand section in place rotate the right-hand section away from you as if to wrap the chain around the bottom of the person's wrist. When the right section has come full circle bring the left section down slightly to the position shown (xxvi).

28. The movement in twenty-seven wraps the chain around the wrist of the opponent, holding it tight. From there

the right-hand continues its anticlockwise rotation and both hands are pushed forward as you step forwards with the right foot (simulating the movement into a figure-four lock with the *nunchaka* and the subsequent takedown) (xxvii).

29. Taking both halves of the *nunchaka* in the right hand (chain above the thumb) lean your body weight back and twist your torso anticlockwise, bringing the *nunchaka* up to perform a cross block (as if from a right punch) (xxviii).

30. Releasing one half of the *nunchaka* flick the *nunchaka* to the right (as if flicking it around the neck of the opponent) and move the left hand over the right arm to catch the loose end (the *nunchaka* at this point would be applying a lock to the opponent's neck) (xxix).

31. Pivot on the right leg and bring the left leg anticlockwise one-quarter of a turn, moving the legs into a body drop position (*see* Chapter 7) (xxx).

32. Now step forward with the right leg pushing the *nunchaka* forward and

(xxiv)

(xxv)

(xxvi)

(xxvii)

(xxviii)

(xxix)

(xxx)

(xxxi)

(xxxii)

(xxxiii)

(xxxiv)

(xxxv)

down at a forty-five degree angle. Both halves should be parallel with the chain tight between them (this is to block a front kick by striking the shin with the chain of the *nunchaka*) (xxxi).

33. Keeping the *nunchaka* parallel bring it up to head height and strike downwards at a forty-five degree angle with the open ends (this is a double strike to the opponent's collar bones) (xxxii).

34. Make a hooking motion with chain of the *nunchaka* (as if to hook the neck of the opponent) (xxxiii).

35. Draw the *nunchaka* down and to the left, lowering the body into a low stance (drawing the opponent down to the ground) and strike forwards with the chain ends of the *nunchaka* to a point just in front of your right foot (xxxiv).

36. Collect both ends of the *nunchaka* in the right hand and stand, turning the torso so that you are in left stance (left foot forward). While doing this bring the left hand up in a guard position (as for two) (xxxv).

37. Place the *nunchaka* back in the belt then bring the right foot up level with the left and finish feet together with hands at the sides.

15 Kneeling *Iai-Jutsu* (Sword)

These six techniques with the *katana* should, at least in part, be familiar to anyone who studies *iaido* (the way of drawing, cutting and then sheathing the sword). The main difference between this and *iai-jutsu* is one of spirit rather than technique (although that too differs, usually arising out of the spiritual differences). So as not to become too philosophical (and vague) the easiest way to explain this is that in *iaido* the opponent is oneself whereas in *iai-jutsu* there is an opponent (imagined or real) external to oneself that you are combating. Donn F. Draeger said it most eloquently stating that the *bu-jutsu* forms are the arts of self-protection whereas the *budo* forms are the art of self-perfection. (*Bu-jutsu* being the martial arts, in terms of combat techniques, and *budo* being the (more holistic) martial ways.)

As with other areas of any martial art there are matters of etiquette to be considered; these vary wildly depending on style and school. In essence the sword is initially carried vertically in the right hand, grasped level with the cord retainer (*kuri-gata*) of the scabbard (*saya*) and with the edge of the blade facing backwards. *Tori* bows, either to his opponent or to the front of the *dojo*, and then transfers the sword to his left hand. In the left hand it is held at the hip, blade edge uppermost, *tori* then kneels and places the sword to his right side, hilt (*tsuka*) facing forwards and with the blade edge towards him. After a kneeling bow *tori* places the sword horizontally in front of him and bows to it. The sword is then slid into the belt at the left hip, blade edge uppermost, and the cord is attached to the belt. In finishing (from kneeling) the sword is again bowed to in front of *tori* then picked up in the left hand and held at the left hip. *Tori* rises to his feet and transfers the sword to the right hand (held as it was in the beginning) and performs a final bow.

This etiquette is deliberately vague due to the wildly varying traditions. The exact position and orientation of the sword varies, where the edge faces and which way to point the hilt. The etiquette is necessary to offer due respect to your sword and opponent (whether this is yourself or another) but if I had to decide I would opt for genuinely expressed respect over the insincere but accurate variety. Because of this I focus more on the techniques.

1. Single Opponent to the Front

Tori starts in a kneeling position (on the toes) with right hand on the thigh and left hand on the mouth of the scabbard (*saya*). *Tori* takes hold of the sword hilt (*tsuka*) in his right hand up against the sword guard (tsuba), the main grip being with the lower three fingers. *Tori* then does three things simultaneously: he rises up on his right leg, turns the scabbard one-quarter of a turn with his left hand so that the edge is facing away from him and starts to draw

Single opponent to the front (start position).

Single opponent to the front (cut across eyes).

Single opponent to the front (return katana along same path).

Single opponent to the front (katana high).

the sword forwards. Once the sword is clear of the scabbard he cuts across horizontally left to right at eye level, stopping at a point about twelve inches beyond where the head would be. He then reverses the path of the blade right to left and brings it over his left shoulder, edge facing backwards, in a defensive position. As this is done he brings the left knee up to just behind the right foot. Continuing the flow of the blade he brings it above his head and takes hold with his left hand at the end of the hilt, then cuts down to level with the abdomen while sliding his right foot forward. *Tori* then twists the blade forty-five degrees and draws back slightly (releasing it from the body) and, letting go with the left hand and placing it on the scabbard mouth, flicks the blade out to the right at shoulder height. *Tori* stands, bringing his left foot up level with his right, and bringing the *katana* up so that the end of the hilt is level with the forehead, blade pointing right (with the blade uppermost). Stepping back with the right foot he flicks the sword down to the right, finishing with the

Single opponent to the front (downward cut).

Single opponent to the front (flick to right).

Single opponent to the front (katana presented).

Single opponent to the front (final flick).

Single opponent to the front (start position for sheathing).

Single opponent to the front (sheathing).

point angled forward (level with his left knee). With his left hand at the mouth of the scabbard, first finger and thumb touching at the back, he brings the *katana* over to rest the back of the blade at the meeting point of the left-hand finger and thumb up near the hilt guard (*tsuba*). Drawing the back of the blade down across the finger and thumb until the point of the blade is in the opening of the scabbard he then re-angles the blade to slide easily into the scabbard. The third and fourth from last photographs are the blood flick (*chiburi*) to clean the blade of unpleasantness; the last two pictures are the sheathing of the blade (*noto*).

2. Opponents to the Front and Rear

The first part of this technique is identical to the first five photographs in the first technique. From there *tori* looks over his left shoulder at the second opponent, brings the *katana* above his head and twists his hips anticlockwise, raising the

Opponents to the front and rear (drop right knee, raise left).

Opponents to the front and rear (downward cut).

Opponents to the front and rear (standing, right leg sideways).

Opponents to the front and rear (present katana).

180

Opponents to the front and rear (flick).

Opponents to the front and rear (sheath).

left knee and dropping the right. From this position *tori* cuts down vertically to the level of the abdomen. After a forty-five degree twist of the blade he stands, stepping forward and to the right with his right foot, and turning ninety degrees to his left, bringing the sword up to his left shoulder. This should place *tori* facing his two opponents and at a right angle to them (ready just in case they survived). The finish is the same as for the first technique; the hilt is brought up level with the forehead and flicked down and to the right, finishing level with the left knee. *Tori* then sheaths the *katana* as previously described.

3. Opponents to the Front and Rear, Reverse Grip

For this technique *tori* twists the scabbard blade out as for the previous two but reverses the grip on the hilt; that is to say that his little finger is now resting next to the guard (*tsuba*) in a similar grip to the ice pick grip shown in Chapter 17. Other than the reverse grip the initial draw and cut is the same as for the previous two techniques, it is just that the palm must be

uppermost to complete the cut across the eyes. *Tori* then needs to bring the sword up over his right shoulder and take hold with his left hand, at the same time bringing his left knee up behind his right foot. He then cuts down vertically to abdomen level (when practising this note the different feel and level of power afforded by this grip). *Tori* then looks over his left shoulder at his second opponent who is standing some way behind him and changes his right hand back to a regular grip. *Tori* then straightens his legs to stand and turns his hips so that he is now in a left stance facing his second opponent with the *katana* in a low stance to his right side. *Tori* brings the *katana* up above his head and steps forward with the right foot, cutting down to chest level. Moving his right foot to the right *tori* turns ninety degrees to the left and brings the *katana* up to the right side. *Tori* then reverses his right hand, returning to the reversed grip he started with, and brings the sword down to his right side, blade pointing backwards and edge downward. *Tori* taps the blade against his right thigh and shakes the blade with a twist of his wrists. Moving the left hand over to hold the end of the scabbard *tori* then steps

181

Opponents to the front and rear, reverse grip (initial cut).

Opponents to the front and rear, reverse grip (downward cut).

Opponents to the front and rear, reverse grip (change of grip, stand looking back, katana high).

Opponents to the front and rear, reverse grip (downward cut to second opponent).

Opponents to the front
and rear, reverse grip
(stepping to the right).

Opponents to the front
and rear, reverse grip
(reverse grip, tap on leg).

Opponents to the front
and rear, reverse grip
(sheathing).

back with the left leg and brings the *katana* over to sheath. This is done as before but as the grip is reversed it may take a little getting used to.

4. Downward Cut, Remaining in Kneeling Position

Unlike the preceding (and following) techniques this one is performed from a kneel-ing position with the feet flat against the ground. *Tori* takes hold of the *katana* in his right hand (regular grip) then rises up on his knees while drawing the sword directly upwards. This will take some slow practice to avoid damage to the scabbard mouth. Once out of the scabbard the sword is brought above the head and the left hand takes hold. *Tori* then cuts down vertically to abdomen level at the same time dropping back into the kneeling

Downward cut remaining kneeling (drawing).

Downward cut remaining kneeling (high position).

Downward cut remaining kneeling (cut).

Downward cut remaining kneeling (strike blade).

Downward cut remaining kneeling
(coming to kneeling, reverse grip).

Downward cut remaining kneeling
(initial sheathing position).

position, thus adding to the speed of the blade. Keeping a loose hold with the left hand pulls the right hand up sharply; this should cause the sword to spin in the left hand getting rid of most of the 'blood'. *Tori* raps the hilt with his right hand then takes hold of the sword with his right hand in a reverse grip and at the same time comes up on his right foot. From here *tori* straightens to a standing position and sheaths the sword as described in the previous technique.

5. Reinforced Side Block

Tori comes up on his right leg and draws the sword halfway out of the scabbard. This is a reinforced block against a horizontal cut to *tori*'s neck. Continuing the drawing of the blade *tori* moves to stand-

ing, pivoting on the right leg and bringing the left leg about forty-five degrees anticlockwise, with the sword above his head in both hands. *Tori* then cuts down across *uke*'s outstretched arms, drawing the sword back to him at the end of the cut. *Tori* then performs a thrust through at chest height. Bending the right arm and bringing the left hand up high *tori* brings the blade to rest across his arm, blade facing *uke*. To complete *tori* moves his left hand to the scabbard and allows the sword to come down in front of him, stopping it sharply, facing forwards and edge-down. *Tori* then rotates the blade clockwise on the outside of his right arm and after one rotation brings the sword up to the scabbard and sheaths it. This finish does take some practise but is quite elegant once it is mastered.

185

Reinforced side block (block).

Reinforced side block (step and draw, cut down across arms).

Reinforced side block (thrust through body).

Reinforced side block (protected position).

Reinforced side block (flick).

Reinforced side block (spin).

6. Horizontal Avoidance Cut

Here *tori* is defending against a downward cut to the head. The first few parts of this technique need to be done simultaneously and do involve a good degree of coordination. *Tori* takes hold of the sword in his right hand and brings his right foot up and to the right; the left hand is again rotating the scabbard so that the sword can come out horizontally. *Tori* continues this motion by rising, pivoting on his right foot and bringing his left foot around in a forty-five degree anticlockwise arc. At the same time *tori* finishes the drawing of the sword and cuts horizontally left to right across *uke*'s abdomen. This first part needs to be done as one flowing motion as this movement avoids *uke*'s attack and causes *uke* to move in to the horizontal cut. After drawing the cut across *uke*, *tori* brings the *katana* back over his left shoulder (defensively, with edge facing backwards) and

Reinforced side block (sheathing position).

Horizontal avoidance cut (move and draw).

Horizontal avoidance cut (cut to body, moving rear leg).

Horizontal avoidance cut (downward cut).

takes hold with his left hand in the high position and then cuts downwards to chest height. The finish is identical as that for the previous technique.

You will notice that it would be possible to finish all six techniques in the same way (as for the first and second technique). The reason I haven't is for variety and practise. It is always nice to know more than one way to do things and it is not for me to say which you might prefer. With this in mind I have described four different finishes spread amongst the techniques but remember: whatever your personal preference it is your responsibility to pass on all the knowledge you can (providing it is not plain daft!) and let your students form their own opinions.

16 *Bo* Work

In this chapter we are looking at the basic use and practice with the *bo*. The *bo* used in ju-jitsu is a staff usually six feet long and just over one inch in diameter. Traditionally it is made of Japanese red oak, making it very durable and quite heavy. Different arts have their own particular sizes and weights (*wing chun* uses a thinner and more flexible staff; its lightness and flexibility is reflected in the way it is used), in *kata* competitions thinner lighter *bo* are used to increase the speed and excitement of the demonstrations. Just as all martial arts have their own particular strengths so do the different sizes of staff and their use.

In this chapter we are showing something called 'walking' the *Bo*. This is a basic *kata* performed in a straight line, forwards and backwards, demonstrating the basic strikes and blocks used.

1. Start position: *bo* held in the right hand (thumb up) vertically at the right side (i).
2. Lean the top of the *bo* forward and take hold with the left hand near the top (thumb down), stepping forward with the left foot (ii).
3. 'Draw the *bo*': extend the left hand forward (arm at shoulder level) and allow the right hand to slide as far back on the *bo* as it can (iii).
4. Bring the right hand up over the head while lowering the left hand and stepping forward with the right leg. As the *bo* is brought down the right hand is slid down to the mid-point and the far end of the *bo* finishes level with the chin. Hand, *bo* and foot should stop as one (iv).
5. 'Draw the *bo*' by moving the left hand as far back as it will go and sliding the

(i)   (ii)

(iii)

(iv)

(v)

(vi)

right hand forwards so again we have the maximum distance between the hands (v).

6. Repeat 4 on the opposite side (forward on the left leg) (vi).

7. 'Draw the *bo*', left arm forward (vii).

8. Stepping forward on the right sweep the right hand down and forward to bring the *bo* in an upwards strike to the groin, allowing the right hand to slide back along the *bo* the halfway point (increasing speed and range of the strike) (viii).

9. 'Draw the *bo*' (DTB hereafter) then step forward with the left and strike upwards to the groin, left hand forward (ix).

10. DTB then bring the *bo* in a horizontal arc up to strike at the side of the head, stepping forward on the right and sliding the right hand down to the mid-point (x).

11. Repeat 10, stepping forwards with the left and striking with the left (xi).

12. DTB then sweep the *bo* horizontally from the right to strike at waist height, stepping in with the right foot and sliding the right hand down to the mid-point (xii).

(vii)

(viii)

(ix)

(x)

(xi)

(xii)

(xiii)

(xiv)

(xv)

(xvi)

13. Repeat 12, stepping forwards with the left foot and striking from the left (xiii).
14. DTB then sweep the *bo* in from the right to strike at the lower leg, stepping in with the right and sliding the right hand to the mid-point of the *bo* (xiv).
15. Repeat 14, stepping forwards with the left foot and striking from the left (xv).

From here we move back and the moves are blocks rather than strikes (although they are very similar).

16. DTB, stepping back with the left foot and sweep the *bo* down from the right side to the lower leg. End position is the same as for 14 (xiv).
17. Repeat 16, stepping back with the right foot and sweeping from the left (xv).
18. DTB stepping back with the left foot and bring the right hand to head height, positioning the *bo* vertically on the left side of the body (xvi).
19. Stepping back with the right foot bring the *bo* to the right side of the body, vertical with the left hand uppermost (xvii).
20. Stepping back with the left foot sweep the *bo* from the right to head height, sliding the right hand down to the mid-point (x).
21. DTB, stepping back with the right. Repeat 20, sweeping from the left (xi).
22. DTB, step back with the left foot and raise the *bo* horizontally above the head (xviii).
23. Bring the right foot back to level with the left, wider than shoulder width, and bring the *bo* down until horizontal (level with mid-thigh), bending the knees slightly (xix).

From there bring the feet together and the *bo* up in the right hand to finish as per 1.

(xvii)

(xviii)

(xix)

17 Use of the *Tanto* (Knife)

The use of the Japanese knife, or *tanto*, is included here for interest's sake only and should only be undertaken at higher levels (second *dan* and beyond). I have described the techniques here but I have deliberately omitted certain aspects of the reasons, exact targets and effects of the strikes. I have also included them as a defence against a thrust to the upper body or face but they are adaptable. Experienced martial artists will understand this omission and those who don't are welcome to come and train at my club where, in the course of your training you will learn the why (by which time you will have earned the right to be taught these aspects). The techniques are shown here using a wooden *tanto* (of a sort used in training).

1. Three Main Grips

Sword Grip
As its name suggests this grip is the same as the basic grip on a sword, with thumb nearest the blade.

Ice Pick Grip
Held as shown here it is mainly for downward stabbing.

Concealed Ice Pick Grip
The hand grip on the knife is the same as for the ice pick grip but the hand is turned slightly so that the back of the blade runs along the inside of the forearm. This is the grip used at the beginning of each of the techniques shown here except the last one.

Sword grip.

Ice pick grip.

Concealed ice pick grip.

2. Upward Cutting Block

With the knife held in a concealed ice pick grip *tori* stands in a slightly modified right stance, the modification being that the right hand is lower than usual. *Uke* attacks with a thrust to the upper body and *tori* moves his left foot to the right slightly (moving his body out of the path of the blade) and brings the knife upwards, cutting on the inside of *uke*'s forearm (left hand kept ready with the back of the wrist facing *uke*'s knife). *Tori* then performs a left to right horizontal cut across *uke*'s neck. *Tori* then does a diagonal cut from upper right to lower left (as *tori* sees it) across *uke*'s chest. Finally *tori* places his left hand at the base of the knife and performs a reinforced thrust to *uke*'s midsection.

This is a combination and can be seen to escalate. The initial cut is painful and potentially disabling; if it is unsuccessful in finishing the encounter it distracts *uke* sufficiently to attempt the second, which is potentially lethal. If *uke* has avoided these *tori* moves onto the third cut, which is again painful or disabling, which leads if necessary to the potentially lethal final cut.

Upward cutting block (block).

Upward cutting block (cut across neck).

Upward cutting block (diagonal cut, top right to bottom left).

Upward cutting block (reinforced thrust).

Downward cutting block (block).

Downward cutting block (diagonal cut, bottom left to top right).

3. Downward Cutting Block

From the modified right stance *uke* attacks with a thrust. *Tori* moves his left leg across to the right and then brings the knife across to cut downwards on the inside of *uke*'s attacking forearm (with the point of the blade pointing upwards). Keeping the left hand in a guard position (because if you are continuing, this person still has a knife in his hand) *tori* turns the knife so that the point of the blade is now pointing down and does a diagonal cut, lower left to upper right, across *uke*'s chest. From the upper point of the diagonal cut *tori*

Downward cutting block (downward thrust).

Upward outside cutting block (block).

Upward outside cutting block (downward pin).

Upward outside cutting block (finish).

reverses the direction and brings the point down at the junction of *uke*'s neck and left shoulder.

4. Upwards Outside Cutting Block

From a left stance *tori* avoids a thrust by stepping forwards and to the left with the left foot and bringing the right leg across to the left, thus placing themselves on the outside of *uke*'s right arm. At the same time *tori* brings the knife, point pointing downwards, up to cut the outside of *uke*'s wrist. *Tori* continues this motion until the blade is clear of *uke*'s wrist then reverses the motion to bring the point down through the wrist. At the same time *tori* hooks his left hand around the far side of *uke*'s neck, tucking the back of his hand under *uke*'s chin, and pulls his hands apart. If necessary *tori* then performs a horizontal cut to the side of *uke*'s neck.

Downward outside cutting block (block).

Downward outside cutting block (butt strike).

5. Downward Outside Cutting Block

As for section four *tori* begins by stepping to the outside of *uke*'s arm, left leg forwards. This time *tori* brings the knife in a downward cut to *uke*'s wrist. *Tori* then strikes under *uke*'s arm to the ribs with the butt of the knife. From there *tori* brings his knife hand up on the inside of *uke*'s arm until the knife rests alongside *uke*'s neck. *Tori* uses his left hand to pull the other side of *uke*'s head so that knife arm and neck are firmly held.

6. Outer Locking Technique

Stepping outwards as for sections four and five *tori* hooks his left arm over *uke*'s right arm (note that the back of the wrist is still facing towards *uke*'s knife) and *tori* turns sharply clockwise, snapping *uke*'s elbow straight against his body. *Tori* continues the rotation of the body and brings the knife

Downward outside cutting block (lock).

199

Outer locking technique (initial block and lock).

Outer locking technique (thrust into back).

into *uke*'s lower back. *Tori* then releases with the left hand (still turning clockwise) and uses it to grab the top of *uke*'s head (preferably the hair). Bringing the knife up *tori* pulls back on the head and cuts across the back of the neck left to right.

7. Wrist Turn Out

Holding the knife in a sword grip, left stance, *tori* steps out with the left leg (right leg following) and does a downward outside parry with the outside of their knife hand. A twist of the wrist brings the blade under *uke*'s wrist, to the inside. *Tori* then takes hold of the back of *uke*'s wrist as for the wrist throw (*see* Chapter 6). From here *tori* twists *uke*'s wrist as if performing the wrist throw one-handed, at the same time drawing the knife back across the wrist. If necessary *tori* can finish off with a thrust while *uke*'s knife hand is restrained.

Outer locking
technique
(finish).

Wrist turn out (wrist take).

Wrist turn out (finish).

18 Basic Unarmed *Kata*

This *kata* is designed to go through a number of parries, strikes and techniques. As I have said previously about all *kata*, it is designed as a way for a student to train solo *in addition* to their regular training. As with all *kata* you need to imagine that you are performing these moves against an opponent and thus your moves should be realistically what you would do if it were a real combat situation. I have kept the descriptions brief here as the parries and strikes are described elsewhere.

1. Step forward with the left leg, left inside forearm parry (i).
2. Step forward with the right, right inside forearm parry (ii).
3. Turn hips anticlockwise, shift weight back, downwards outside forearm parry (iii).
4. Step back with the right foot, weight on the back foot, left downwards outside forearm parry (for 3 and 4 parry as for defences against kicks described in Chapter 12) (iv).

(i)

(ii)

(iii)

(iv)

(v)

(vi)

(vii)

(viii)

(ix)

5. Step back on the left leg, cross block with the right arm (v).
6. Backfist (directed where the face of the person you just blocked would be) (vi).
7. Leave feet in position and turn body anticlockwise to face back 180 degrees, left downward inside forearm parry (defending against a right front snap kick) and an upward hooking motion with the left arm (vii).
8. Move forward with the right foot then perform a right knife hand to front of neck (backhanded), and sweep with the right leg (xviii).
9. Stamp with right foot (to the groin of the opponent just thrown) (ix).
10. Right outside forearm parry (as if from a punch coming from the left) (x).
11. Left knife hand to the left (striking at the neck of the person just parried) (xi).

(x)

(xi)

12. Left arm in an anticlockwise circle (encircling the opponent's neck) (xii).
13. In this position drop down on the right knee (arm and possibly neck break) (xiii).
14. Both hands flat on head (defending against a hair grab) (xiv).
15. Keeping hands on head and feet in position stand and turn 180 degrees clockwise (xv).
16. Left front snap kick to the hair puller and remain in left stance (xvi).
17. Right front snap kick and step out to the right with the foot (xvii).
18. Arms and legs positioned as for a drawing ankle (*see* Chapter 7) (xviii).
19. Turn ninety degrees clockwise and right stamp to the floor (to the head of the person thrown) (xix).
20. Step back with the left foot, left hand to left shoulder (as if pushed), right palm heel to attacker (xx).

(xii)

(xiii)

(xiv)

(xv)

(xvi)

(xvii)

(xviii)

21. Reach over to the right shoulder as if grabbing for the wrist lock (*see* Chapter 7, lock 9(i)) (xxi).
22. Turn the upper body ninety degrees clockwise, bringing both hands up to form the lock mentioned in 21. (xxii).
23. Double palm heel strike to the wrist-locked opponent (xxiii).
24. Look back over right shoulder and turn the hips so that you are now facing an opponent behind you (right stance) and perform a downwards palm heel parry (kick from the right) (xxiv).
25. Move the right foot towards the opponent just parried and right elbow in that direction (xv).
26. Turn to face 180 degrees from the target of the elbow and bring right knee up (xvi).
27. From this position continue into a left stance a side thrust kick (in the

(xix)

(xx)

opposite direction to the elbow in 25) (xxvii).

28. Put the right foot down and turn ninety degrees anticlockwise (now in left stance facing the original direction) and perform an upwards X block (xxviii).

29. Draw onto the right knee (xxix).

30. Left hand down, right hand up (neck twist) and feet together with hands at the side to finish (xxx).

(xxi)

(xxii)

(xxiii)

(xxiv)

(xxv)

(xxvi)

(xxvii)

(xxviii)

(xxix)

(xxx)

19 Ju-Jitsu and the Law

This is just a brief look at the law (in the United Kingdom) and how it affects ju-jitsu. The two main areas I am going to mention are the use of ju-jitsu techniques and the carrying of weapons.

The first comes under the broad heading of the use of force. In law an assault is defined as anything that causes another person to apprehend immediate and unlawful violence (from *Fagan* vs. *Metropolitan Police Commissioner*, 1968). The various different assault offences are merely qualifications of this definition (either by the level of injury caused or by the intent). With any use of ju-jitsu we seek to eliminate one aspect of this initial definition and thus eliminate any offence. The aspect we seek to eliminate is the 'unlawful' part.

One instance where use of violence is deemed to be lawful is something we use whenever we train: consent. Be careful with this part though; a person can only consent to *reasonable* violence (I use that word for ease not accuracy). The more important instances where violence is not deemed to be unlawful are in matters of defence.

Three main pieces of legislation cover the lawful use of force: section 117 of the Police And Criminal Evidence Act 1984, section three of the Criminal Law Act and common law. I will not go into unnecessary detail with the relevant acts and sections, but they can be easily summarized. A person is allowed to use force in a few main areas: in defence of themselves; in

defence of another; in defence of their property and to effect or assist in a lawful arrest. The last of these I am not going to go into because it is unlikely you will come across this situation (unless it is part of your day-to-day work, in which case it would be redundant to explain).

The three remaining situations for defence are covered by two huge caveats; the force used must be *reasonable* and *proportionate*. This is something which only requires common sense: is it reasonable to kick someone full force in the groin because they looked at you in a funny way? Ninety-nine per cent of the time the obvious answer, no, is correct. On the one per cent where the 'funny' look was a prelude to the person taking out a knife and trying to kill you then yes, it was reasonable.

I cannot give you an answer to every situation because of the 'what if' factor. The easiest way to work out if something is reasonable and proportionate is to think how a normal person on the street would view the situation if it were explained to them. A reasonable person would undoubtedly agree that an armlock put on with full force was a reasonable response to a knife attack. Consider though that this same person would probably not consider your response proportionate if, following this defence, the attacker turned to run away and you continued hitting them, or if you picked up the knife and stabbed them in the back.

Hopefully you are getting the idea; in an ideal world you evaluate (probably on a subconscious level) the attack and respond at a similar level of force (minor force right up to deadly force). In this ideal world you would re-evaluate whether to continue after each use of force and, if the threat is no longer there, stop.

I cannot stress this enough: you must always be ready to stand by your actions and justify them. If you use a level of force and feel uncomfortable trying to defend it then it was probably not reasonable and proportionate. At the end of the day your conscience is your guide.

One last thing about defending yourself; consider this opinion of mine: I would far rather defend my actions in a court of law than through a medium!

The carrying of weapons is an area of the law I get asked about more than any other. First and foremost I would say that if you are below eighteen years of age and want to practise with weapons then borrow them from your *sensei*. For everyone else there are two main areas of law to consider; possession of an offensive weapon and possession of a bladed or sharply pointed object (in a public place).

The second of the two speaks for itself but the first one I will explain. An offensive weapon is defined as any item that is made, adapted or intended to cause injury. As you can see martial arts weapons tend to fall into one of these categories.

As with use of force I will just concentrate on the defences to having such items. The first such defence does not apply within martial arts and this is the defence of lawful authority. This applies to police officers, the armed forces and so on (not to security guards I'm afraid). The other, and

more important, defence is that of reasonable excuse. These can be numerous, involving religious observation, national dress, camping and other such things but for martial arts it is simpler. The reasonable excuse is that you are carrying the item to or from a training session (or from the place you bought it of course). So as long as you have the item carefully wrapped in your bag and can show that you are going to or coming from a session, then no problem. The upshot of this is that you should never forget to take them out of your vehicle when not doing either of these two journeys. You may be able to defend your possession of them, but it is harder.

One last point about weapons; there are a small group of weapons that are always offensive weapons and for which there is no reasonable excuse to have them (except for taking them to a police station because you have just found them). There is quite a list of these, a couple of examples are the *balisong* (butterfly knife) and *shuriken* (throwing stars). The easy way to avoid trouble is not to buy any weapon without first asking your *sensei*. Another way is to buy only from reputable dealers, as it is an offence to sell such weapons. Be careful of buying interesting-looking weapons abroad because other countries do not have the same restrictions as Britain and you may well be falling foul of this law. This is only sensible; after all, you wouldn't buy a gun in America and expect to be able to bring it into this country would you?

I hope this clears up some points, if in doubt just pop into your local library or police station and ask. Questions are never a problem; trying to plead ignorance can be!

20 And Finally

I hope I have given you a small insight into ju-jitsu or, if you already have some experience of it, that I have given you something to take away with you. As I said at the beginning this is only an overview and, if you are interested, you have a world of further reading ahead. The one thought I will leave you with is this: never be satisfied!

By all means enjoy the satisfaction of achievement but never believe that there is nothing else to achieve. Every serious martial artist continues to try and improve their art as long as they are able to continue. Consider that even Bruce Lee was not satisfied and, had he lived today, I am positive he would still be looking at ways to improve himself. He was the sort of warrior that comes along once in an age, and if he still looked to improve himself the rest of us could do worse than to follow his example.

Try as many martial arts as you can and enjoy every second. The martial art that you enjoy most is probably the one you are best suited to, but don't be satisfied with that. That martial art is the starting point for developing your personal martial art. Martial arts started because a person found a way of fighting that worked for them and passed it on. Unless you are identical to that person in every way you need to adapt what you learn so that it works for you.

Have fun!

Appendix – Targets

Here I have just shown some of the main *atemi* points on the body, there are far more than this! I have named the targets and I have denoted them hard (H), semi-hard (SH) and soft (S) (something you can probably work out for yourself). I have not included the effect of the strike. This bit of information I am reluctant to put in a book that is open for anyone to read. This is not because of any desire to be mysterious; this is an act of responsibility. Any *sensei* worth their salt will assess their student to find out if they are responsible enough (and have the self-control) to handle this information. This part, for non-practitioners, is of academic interest only, for practitioners it is a handy reference.

Front

1. Temple (SH).
2. Eye (S).
3. Ear (SH).
4. Jaw hinge (S for the muscle and nerve, H for the bone).
5. Hollow behind jaw (S for nerve).
6. Nerve under jaw line (S).
7. Brachial plexus origin, jugular vein, carotid artery (S for nerve and blood flow, SH for neck).
8. Side of and behind throat (S).
9. Frontal bone (H).
10. Nose (S).
11. Upper jaw (S for nerve, H for bone).
12. Lower jaw (S for nerve as shown, H for bone).
13. Front of throat (S).
14. Supra scapular (SH due to heavy muscle).
15. Jugular notch (just above the sternum) (S).
16. Subclavian nerve (S).
17. Clavicle (SH).
18. Shoulder hollow (SH for nerve).
19. Sternum (H).
20. Lymph glands (armpit) (S).
21. Ribs (SH for true and false ribs, S for floating).
22. Solar plexus (S).
23. Bicep (inside of the arm between the bicep and bone) (S).
24. Forearm nerve (radial) (S).
25. Pelvis (S for pain compliance up to H for the bone).
26. Groin (S).
27. Common perennial nerve (SH due to muscle size).
28. Anterior femoral nerve (SH).
29. Lateral femoral nerve (SH).
30. Knee (H).
31. Shin (H).
32. Metatarsals (SH).

Front illustration

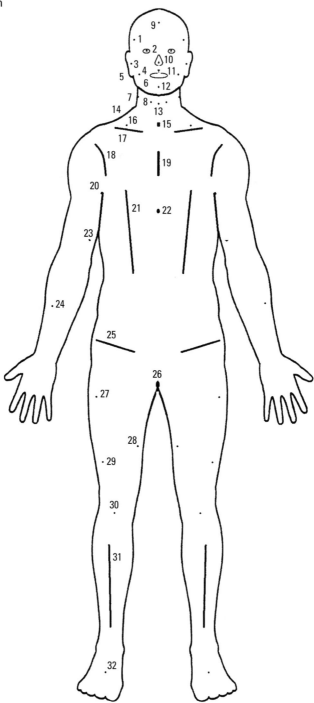

Rear illustration

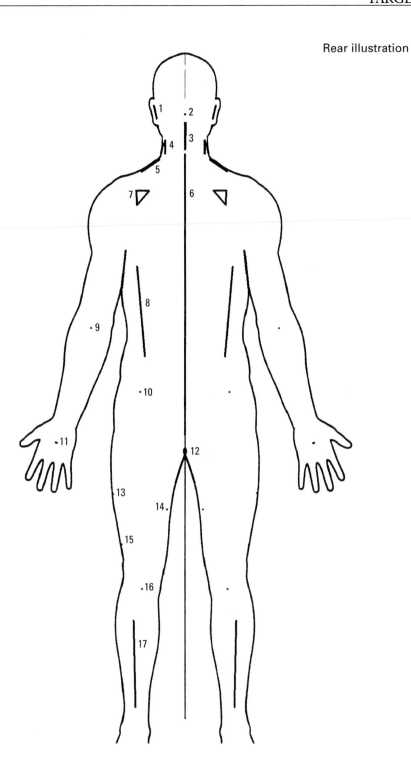

Rear

1. Ear (SH).
2. Medulla oblongata (SH).
3. Spine (neck area) (SH).
4. Neck (as 7 for the front).
5. Supra scapular (SH).
6. Spine (H).
7. Scapular (H).
8. Ribs (as 21 for the front).
9. Elbow (H).
10. Kidneys (SH).
11. Metacarpals (back of hand) (SH).
12. Coccyx (base of the spine) (H).
13. Common perennial nerve (SH due to muscle size).
14. Anterior femoral nerve (SH).
15. Lateral femoral nerve (SH).
16. Rear of knee (SH).
17. Calf muscle (SH).

Further Reading

I have only included a few books on this list. This is because my advice is to read as many books as you can on any subject that interests you: a comprehensive reading list would therefore look like the British Library catalogue! If you are interested in ju-jitsu then read all the books you can find on the subject.

That said I have included a few books that, although not specifically about ju-jitsu, do fall into my 'if you read nothing else' category:

Lee, B., *Tao of Jeet Kune Do* (Ohara Publications, 1992).

Draeger, D.F. and Warner, G., *Japanese Swordsmanship* (Weatherhill Inc., 1991).

Draeger, D.F., *Classical Bujutsu*, Martial Arts and Ways of Japan Series Vol. I (Weatherhill Inc., 1996).

Finn, M., Iaido: *The Way of the Sword* (Paul H. Crompton, 1982).

Musashi, M., *A Book of Five Rings* (Allison and Busby, 2004).

Tzu, S., *The Art of War* (Hodder and Stoughton, 1988).

Index